Surviving the
Credit Crunch
of the '90s

Surviving the Credit Crunch of the '90s

Rescuing Your Small Business
from Meltdown
and Making It A Success

Lance H. Woeltjen
President
Virtual Realities Laboratories, Inc.

Thomas B. Sanders
Assistant Professor of Finance
University of Southern Maine—Portland

Chilton Book Company
Radnor, Pennsylvania

Copyright © 1991 by Lance H. Woeltjen and Thomas B. Sanders

All Rights Reserved

Published in Radnor, Pennsylvania 19089, by Chilton Book Company

No part of this book may be reproduced, transmitted or stored in any form or by any means, electronic or mechanical, without prior written permission from the publisher

Designed by Jerry O'Brien
Manufactured in the United States of America

Library of Congress Cataloging in Publication Data
Woeltjen, Lance H.
    Surviving the credit crunch of the '90s: rescuing your small business and making it a success / Lance H. Woeltjen, Thomas B. Sanders.
        p.   cm.
    Includes index.
    ISBN 0-8019-8015-1
    1. Small business—United States—Finance.   I. Sanders, Thomas B.
II. Title.
HG4027.7.W64   1990
658.15'92—dc20   90-55319
                                                                          CIP

Readers wishing to contact the authors can write or telephone: Lance Woeltjen, 2341 Ganador, San Luis Obispo, CA 93401; or Tom Sanders, University of Southern Maine, School of Business, Portland, ME 04103, 207/883-8694.

1 2 3 4 5 6 7 8 9 0   9 8 7 6 5 4 3 2 1

For
Bonny and Susie

Contents

Contents

Contents

Contents

Contents

Acknowledgments

We are especially grateful to Bryan Milling for his helpful comments on the early phases of this book. Douglas B. Chaffee, William H. Nikkel, John J. Gardiner III, and John J. Mehalchin all provided important practical tools and lessons in small business financial management. We would also like to thank Thomas Adelman of Immucell Corp.; Charlton Ames of Morse, Payson & Noyes; William Aron of J. T. Moran & Co.; Christine Cyr; Alan Jeffryes of Alan C. Jeffreyes & Co.; John Lincoln of Ventrex Laboratories; Katherine Regan of Tucker Anthony, Inc; Rodney Small of Country Business, Inc.; Steven Thing, CPA; and Scott Weismann of Kelly, Drye & Warren.

Preface

The 1980s witnessed the formation of an unprecendented number of new businesses, and small businesses accounted for the great majority of all new jobs created. But the same decade witnessed record-breaking rates of bankruptcy. In fact, the rate of small business failure rose more rapidly than the rate of new business formation.

Why the distressingly high number of bankruptcies among small businesses?

One major reason lies in a fundamental difference between running a small business and running a big one. Many of those middle managers freed during the recent rash of corporate mergers and white-collar layoffs have become independent entrepreneurs. Managers from big companies find the small business environment much different than the large corporate world they're used to, and they are surprised at the difficulties they encounter. While some new ventures prosper, the vast majority experience serious, seemingly irreversible, financial troubles. The causes of the troubles always differ, but the problems always manifest themselves eventually as a cash crisis.

During the 1980s, conventional wisdom held that cash shortages stemmed from undercapitalization. However, a more frequent problem was lack of appreciation by big-company alumni of the key role of cash in the success of a small business. Liberalized bankruptcy laws also made it easier for owners to choose bankruptcy rather than undertake the hard work necessary to turn a company around.

Surviving the Credit Crunch of the '90s tells you how to avoid bankruptcy and turn your troubled company into a profitable business.

Other small business financial self-help books discuss how to get into business but not how to survive the financial woes that commonly lead to failure among new and even more-seasoned small businesses. Other books' discussions of raising capital often gloss over the *informal* capital market and concentrate on professional venture capital. The reader is often left with the wrong conclusion that professional venture capital is easily accessible. In reality, professional venture capital is obtained by very few new companies. The vast majority of capitalization is done through the informal market.

Furthermore, other books do not yield an integrated picture of how to

- stop a credit meltdown (the path to bankruptcy)
- turn the company around
- plan for growth within cash constraints
- raise capital
- sell a company at a profit

Surviving the Credit Crunch of the '90s fills that void.

The idea for a book on how to turn a small company around, expand it, and sell it, evolved as a series of discussions between its authors. We saw the need for a practical self-help financial guide for the owner of a business with sales from $1 to $5 million per year. Frequently, companies with annual sales of less than $5 million cannot afford management depth in finance. *Surviving the Credit Crunch of the '90s* combines our considerable practical and academic financial experience in a way that makes our expertise easily accessible to the layman.

Since the goal of the book is to be a financial road map for small businesses stalled on the expressway to the American Dream, the book follows a progression from near disaster to realization of the Dream. The book begins with a rescue operation—saving the small company faced with imminent credit meltdown. The initial four chapters deal with turning around a company in crisis. Chapter 1 addresses the problem of regaining cash control on an emergency basis, and Chapter 2 shows how to analyze what business practices led to the crisis. Chapter 3 is on how to plan achievable goals through financial forecasting, and Chapter 4 is on how to control the company once it is stabilized. It addresses the steps that are necessary to assure that the company doesn't falter again because of inadequate financial control.

Chapters 5, 6, 7 are devoted to new product or new business start-up. Turnaround alone won't guarantee the success of the renewed company. It can't assure ongoing survival in the dynamic business world. New ideas, new products, and growth in new market segments are the engine for long-term success in an increasingly competitive world and they are the precondition to successful sale for most small businesses. The growth cycle has three parts: planning for a new product or company, raising capital for it, and nurturing it to the critical breakeven point. Most of Chapters 5, 6, and 7 are related to a new business start-up because a turnaround company requires a few years to regain its credibility. If a going concern has never suffered a collapse, much of Chapters 5, 6, and 7 may be applied to new product financing.

Entrepreneurs would like to be rewarded for the large risks they take and for their heavy personal investment in a private business. That reward is usually measured in financial success and the ability to harvest enough gain at the end of a successful career to retire independently. Thus Chapters 8 and 9, the last two chapters of the book, are on how to realize ultimate success by selling a small company for a significant amount of money through a broker or through a public offering.

Surviving the Credit Crunch of the '90s teaches you how to rescue, refloat, and sell a firm that was once on the brink of failure. It provides a valuable, comprehensive resource not previously available in a single volume.

C H A P T E R 1

Regaining
Emergency
Cash Control

In this chapter you will see how Jake, the CEO of Superdisk, Inc., a hypothetical small manufacturing company, regains control in a cash crisis. We assume that he knows a considerable amount about how the company got into cash trouble, but he does not have a finance background, so he is undergoing a learning process where financial concepts and tools are described and where he learns how to use his management skills to apply them to the problem.

We will show how Jake finds money by putting off luxury payables and negotiating "debt switching" arrangements. Jake will attempt to get payment from one of his customers who is on the brink of failure and will observe what could happen to Superdisk if he were to let a credit meltdown occur. *A credit melt-down occurs when a company does not have enough money to pay all creditors and must pay COD (or in advance) for key supplies. This use of cash means less is available to pay overdue bills, and the situation feeds upon itself until all credit it lost.* Once credit meltdown starts, it goes to completion very rapidly, which is why a term analogous to a nuclear power plant meltdown is so appropriate.

Jake will pick up additional cash by collecting his receivables more diligently, and he will learn a variety of ways to mine his inventory for cash. He will take an immediate strategic action by reducing the number of his employees. He will orchestrate all these activities with a simple cash flow control spreadsheet. When you are finished with this chapter, you will understand how to regain control of cash and maintain credit on an emergency basis.

The CEO Must Control the Cash

Who bears the responsibility for stopping cash outflow? It must be the CEO. If it is not currently the CEO, chief executive, the CEO must get the reins back in his own hands. The CEO must control all expenditures in order to regain control of cash in an emergency.

Let's consider the hypothetical case of Superdisk, Inc., a rapidly growing manufacturer of optical disk drives for data storage. At Superdisk, let us assume that the CEO, Jake, is an expert engineer and a world-renowned authority on computer format standards. In order to give his company the credibility that it needs to be successful in the marketplace, Jake must travel to Europe and Japan and meet frequently with international standards committees. He has a good accountant, Joan, in charge of paying suppliers, and Bob, the manager of his purchasing department, has ten years of experience. Jake is good at delegation. He believes in hiring top people, giving them a lot of individual responsibility, and helping them only to the extent of giving them the resources they need to do their jobs. After all, if they can't handle payables, collections, and purchase orders, how is the boss going to have time to do their work and his own too?

Jake is correct to delegate, as long as Superdisk is operating with sufficient cash. But its cash has been chronically strained to the limit, and Superdisk has been ruining its credit standing by failing to pay its suppliers. Since there is a cash crisis at Superdisk, there is nothing more important than for Jake to get it under control as swiftly as possible. Otherwise, the company will fail. For the sake of our illustration, assume the cash crisis at Superdisk has been going on for some time now, and Joan, the accountant, while keeping Jake informed, has tried to shield him from the full brunt of angry supplier phone calls.

What should Jake do first? First, he must assume personal control of all expenditures. He must sign every check, every purchase order, and require all credit cards be returned to his pocket. He has to control the expenditure of every cent in a cash emergency. He is going to have to decide what needs to be paid. He can't afford to be ignorant of cash decisions being made contrary to his plans, and he can't afford to delegate control of expenditures until the emergency is under control. Second, he should make certain that all his managers are aware of what he is doing.

The strategy for handling vendors before a credit meltdown occurs is much different than after a credit meltdown. After a credit meltdown, a company is on a cash-only basis with its suppliers. They will require a clearing out of existing debt or progress on that debt before shipping the supplies needed to stay in business. In the case of Superdisk, the company has not yet entered meltdown. Jake will uncover this fact in his research.

What's Accounting's Story?

At Superdisk, payment priority has been done on an ad hoc basis. Jake has received calls from vendors who claim that Joan has lied to them about when they would be paid. Worse yet, Jake has heard from his own marketing and purchasing managers, Maura and Bob, that Joan has lied to them about when a Superdisk sales representative and the single-source coatings suppliers were to be paid. Still worse, Jake has already called in the accountant twice and lectured her about living up to her word and not promising unless she can deliver.

Once again, Jake calls in Joan to let her know that vendors rely upon the absolute integrity of her commitments and that changing or abandoning those commitments must stop.

"Joan, Ace Steel just called and said that you had lied about putting their check in the mail last Friday. Maura tells me that you lied about paying our rep in Atlanta last week. But, worst of all, Bob tells me that you stiffed Rainbow Coatings! Don't you know we're dead if we don't have those coatings on the line by next week?"

Remember, Joan has been trying to shield her boss from the full impact of how bad things are in payables. She doesn't want to be a whiner, but she is losing the trust of suppliers and fellow employees.

"Look, Jake, I've really had it with Maura and Bob. I gave them a 'best estimate' date for payment and they passed it along as a firm commitment. My payables clerk told Rainbow Coatings that they would be paid and didn't bother to call them back when I decided to hold all payments until the big check from Lockheed came in. You were the one who told me we had to pay the health insurance! You can't have it both ways! I'm sorry, but I'm fed up with being told that I'm lying to people! I quit!"

This mock drama illustrates why Jake should have reviewed payment priorities *before* they became a crisis. The accountant or payables clerk has no way of understanding broad corporate financial strategy. He or she may make mistakes in setting priorities and pay those vendors who complain most frequently.

Nobody other than the CEO can determine the full range of cash priorities in a cash crisis. Until cash is once again under control, by definition, there won't be enough to meet all demands. Therefore, the CEO must control the cash.

After thinking about it, Jake realized that his accounting department, although in disarray, was a strong asset. He called Joan back, apologized, and asked her to stay on.

The second thing that Jake did was to get Joan to open up and tell him the whole story. He listened and took copious notes. Then he interviewed his entire accounting staff and took even more notes. Jake knew that his first priority was to determine whether or not a meltdown of vendor credit had occurred. In a meltdown situation, vendor credit is withdrawn. Before meltdown, the withdrawal of credit is merely threatened.

Identifying Unused Borrowing Capacity

A business that has used up its "cash capability" (cash capability = unused borrowing capacity + cash on hand) will be destroyed by a credit meltdown. Cash capability defines the maximum amount of cash available to a company. If current cash requirements exceed cash capability, by definition a company is in a cash crisis, but not necessarily in a meltdown.

First, Jake will investigate the unused borrowing capacity portion of the cash capability equation. Later he will investigate Superdisk's accounts receivable and inventory, looking for ways in which to convert those assets into cash, thereby increasing Superdisk's cash capability.

Unused borrowing capacity is the most ready source of cash. It is composed of unused bank credit or other unused sources of loans and unused credit available from vendors. A meltdown or withdrawal of vendor credit will have an immediate large-scale negative effect on borrowing capacity and, therefore, on cash capability. Withdrawal of unused vendor credit will reduce a company's cash capability dollar for dollar.

Jake will ask Joan to provide an accurate accounts payable aging report so he can form a strategy making maximum use of Superdisk's credit, while assuming that he doesn't create a situation where Superdisk's credit is withdrawn.

What the Accounts Payable Aging Report Reveals

An accounts payable aging report shows how much is owed to each vendor and for how long. It will often contain vouching information (accounting will "vouch" each bill to make certain that it is due, *i.e.,* that the items billed were ordered, received, inspected, accepted, and not yet paid for), and it may or may not contain vendor billing invoice numbers.

If a company has been managing its accounting informally, as is often the case with small businesses, it should immediately begin to produce a monthly financial statement, accounts receivable aging, and accounts payable aging. Basic financials and aging reports can be produced inexpensively by most bookkeepers and all accountants. These basic accounting tools are mandatory in order to regain control of cash in a cash crisis.

If Jake is to rescue Superdisk's credit while in the midst of a cash crunch, he must begin by analyzing his accounts payable aging (Table 1–1).

The first thing that stands out in the accounts payable aging is the "Total" line. The "over 60 day" column is bloated, and the "over 90 day" column, which is normally empty except for the disputes, shows substantial problems. Abex Screw, Arnold's Elec-

TABLE 1–1

Accounts Payable Aging Report
12–17–90 Posting

Vendor	Current	Over 30	Over 60	Over 90
Abex Screw Co.	7,287.80	13,518.70	7,675.85	27,046.50
Arnold's Electric	1,755.00	3,777.15	2,933.45	5,989.75
German Engines	4,109.95	26,267.80		
Drales Water Van	715.00	1,430.00	1,430.00	2,860.00
Lone Star Florist	1,137.50			
Mercury Switches			7,424.30	58,451.25
Rainbow Coatings	51,349.35	152,488.70	382,785.65	
Silver Wire, Inc.	2,751.45	5,734.30	4,232.15	
Titanium Tooling	2,050.75	6,650.15		
Vanadium Supply, Ltd.			80,317.90	
Zeno's Office Products	3,647.15			
Total	74,803.95	209,866.80	486,799.30	94,347.50

tric, and Drales Water Van all show normal monthly amounts until the "over 90" column where they almost double. This probably means these accounts have some items "over 120." They are near meltdown. Another supplier, Mercury Switches, may have already withdrawn credit, since there was no activity in the last 60 days.

Further review shows that Titanium Tooling, where Jake has the company plane maintained and overhauled, is fairly current. The reason is that the owner reminds Jake of his tab, and Jake reminds accounting, which kept it current. Lone Star Florist is a similar account. In this case, Jake's wife orders gifts and flowers for company holidays on credit. She's particularly sensitive to keeping this account up to date because it's run by a friend in town. The Drales Water Van account is for bottled water for the coffee machine. It became excessively aged because the water company never complained. Finally, there was the German Engines account which had been dramatically increased recently in order to rebuild the company Porche and Mercedes.

Jake knows that Abex Screw is the least expensive source for fasteners and that his production will shut down without fasteners. Rainbow Coatings sells a proprietary magnetic coating for his disk drives. They are a sole source, and a second supplier could take months to acquire. Silver Wire sells a necessary commodity that can be purchased elsewhere. Vanadium Supply is another critical account. Although he only purchases Vanadium once every three or four months, there is no substitute for the material in his manufacturing process. Finally, Zeno's Office Products is current because the accountant makes those purchases.

Setting Vendor Payment Priorities

The first step Jake will take is to cut off payments on all luxuries. Titanium Tooling, Drales Water Van, German Engines, and Lone Star Florists are put on "payment hold" and no further purchases will be made there until Superdisk is back to business as usual.

In addition, since they are not a sole source, he asks Joan to let Zeno's account age to "over 60."

Getting rid of the luxuries, and taking more time to pay the noncritical accounts will yield about $50,000 to be applied elsewhere. (Titanium Tooling, Drales Water Van, Lone Star Florist, and German Engines are put on payment hold, providing $46,650.15 over the next 60 days, and Zeno's will be allowed to age to over 60 days, providing another $3,647.15 for a total of $50,297.30 temporarily available that would have otherwise been paid.) With these first decisions, Jake has made $50,000 cash temporarily available. He will reallocate a little more than $33,000 immediately to Abex and Arnold's to bring them back down to "over 60."

Jake still has major problems with Rainbow Coatings and Vanadium Supply. He doesn't need to pay immediately, but within a few days those accounts will go "over 90" if he can't come up with $463,104 ($382,785.65 + $80,317.90). At this point the president of Mercury Switches calls to say he will sue if he doesn't get immediate payment of the $65,875.55 owed Mercury. Jake talks to him for a while, tells him about how he is growing and has run into a temporary cash bind, and offers to start sending $26,000 a month until he has paid off the total debt. In return, Mercury Switches says that it will open his current account and allow him to charge up to the amount that he pays down the old debt. In the trade that is known as rotating or switching old debt for new, and it is one of the important strategies for reestablishing credit after a meltdown (which is exactly what was happening to the Mercury Switches account until Jake intervened).

Jake still has $17,000 ($50,000 made available less $33,000 redirected to Abex and Arnold's) to temporarily reallocate. The deal with Mercury Switches didn't use any cash, since it reopened Superdisk's ability to charge the amount that he repays on the old debt. In reviewing accounts payable and seeing that they are near meltdown and in hearing complaints about payments from vendors and employees, it is obvious to Jake that there is major cash flow trouble at Superdisk in the next few weeks which $17,000 is not going to alleviate.

Since Jake will come up short without a more comprehensive search for cash, he decides to make a cash budget to see where cash is coming from, and where it is going.

Using the Emergency Cash Budget

Jake understands that the old, informal way of budgeting isn't going to work when resources are slim and when promises are being made that are dependent upon each other. He asks Joan for a very simple emergency cash budget to let him keep track of cash detail as he takes the actions necessary to regain cash control. To produce an emergency cash budget, Joan must begin with a starting cash position, add planned deposits, and subtract planned payments to yield budgeted ending cash position. Many households use this same method to make certain they don't overdraw the family checking account. A manufacturing company is more complex, but the same principles apply.

Based upon experience, Joan knows an emergency cash budget should forecast five weeks into the future. This way a company has a full five weeks to prepare for its monthly expenditures. The forecast is rerun once a week, adding the past week to history and a new week to the end of the forecast period. (The emergency cash budget in Table 1–2) is shortened to only two weeks and one day to make the example easier to follow.)

The forecast should account for each day, since that is how a company receives and disburses funds during a cash crisis.

There is little mystery to a cash budget. Referring to Table 1–2, Joan's first step is to provide from the balanced checking account a starting cash-on-hand of $15,275 for today, 1-02-91. Next she listed the items that will add to Superdisk's cash over the next five weeks and the items that will decrease cash during the same period. All the items from "starting cash" through "bank draw" are additions to cash. "Payroll" through "payment on credit line" are dele-

9

TABLE 1-2

Emergency Cash Budget

	1-02-91	1-03-91	1-04-91	1-05-91	1-06-91	1-09-91	1-10-91	1-11-91	1-12-91	1-13-91
Starting Cash	15,275.00	116,238.75	−31,296.30	12,578.70	−66,296.85	−66,296.85	288,329.75	288,329.75	288,329.75	351,704.75
Cash additions										
Flettner Drives		4,949.75								
H. Moxness				1,442.35						
Subatu		36,075.00								
ABC		6,440.20								
Danborough						629,112.25				
Wisc. Salami										5,669.95
Wisc. Salami										2,338.05
Scrap sale			4,875.00							
Sale of CNC lathe			39,000.00							
Sale of press										2,000.00
Tax refund									63,375.00	
Bank draw	160,000.00									
Cash deletions										
Payroll										
Merc Switch	−26,000.00									
Abex Screw	−27,046.50									
Rainbow Coatings		−195,000.00				−187,785.65				
Arnold's Electric	−5,989.75									
Vanadium Supply				−80,317.90		−67,200.00				
Payroll tax										
Rent										
Utilities										
Insurance										
Payment on credit line						−19,500.00				−224,000.00
Ending Cash	116,238.75	−31,296.30	12,578.70	−66,296.85	−66,296.85	288,329.75	288,329.75	288,329.75	351,704.75	137,712.75

10

tions from cash. Notice the specific description of each cash transaction. When the life of a company is on the line, it is well to be very specific.

From the previous analysis of payables aging, Jake can now see on Table 1–2 the required payments to sole sources, Abex and Arnold's, for $27,046.50 and $5,989.75. He can also see the agreed-upon monthly payment of $26,000 to Mercury. Since Rainbow Coatings is due within a few days, to prevent "over 90" status, Jake plans to request two payments of $195,000 and $187,785.65. Finally, an $80,317.90 check must be mailed to Vanadium Supply by 1-05-91.

Tomorrow Jake will look for the incoming Subatu payment of $36,075 before releasing the first check to Rainbow Coatings. Otherwise he will wait another day. The same is true of Vanadium Supply, which will also be floated.

Using Float

Float is a way to "find" cash for a few days since checks drawn today are not cleared for a few days, which means Jake has use of the cash for those days. (Caution: float should be used only temporarily and in emergencies, never routinely; it should be used only against payments that are sure to come in on a specific date. *Often the payer can be instructed to wire transfer funds to the company bank account to be sure of their receipt on a certain date.*)

Following the rule of floating outgoing checks only against assured receipts, Jake decided to float the Abex Screw and Arnold's Electric checks for two days. Both checks were mailed 1-02-91 to out-of-town suppliers. Although the emergency cash budget shows ending cash of minus $31,296.30 on 1-03-91, the sum of the floated Arnold's and Abex checks is $33,036.25, which is enough to keep Superdisk's checking balance positive. These checks were floated against the "sure" payments from Subatu and sale of the CNC lathe. Similarly, Jake floats the Vanadium Supply check from 1-05-91 to 1-09-91 knowing that the

Danborough payment is due by wire on the first day the Vanadium Supply check can possibly clear.

Recording Cash Decisions

Jake realizes it is a good practice to always make a record of promises to pay and payment instructions that are given to the accounting staff. Payment instructions become part of the emergency cash forecast and are placed in a tickler file, so that promises are kept. The tickler file can be a simple three-ring notebook in which special payment instructions are organized by promise dates. Although accounting is writing the physical checks, Jake signs them. When the payment that was promised is sent, he simply removes it from the tickler file. Such "special arrangement" payments are never delegated in an emergency cash management mode.

Now that Jake has several places to record his cash decisions (a written record of promises and an emergency cash budget), he can turn to finding more cash by determining Superdisk's unused borrowing capacity as a part of overall cash capability.

Establishing Maximum Cash Capability

The $17,000 that Jake "found" in taking charge of his accounts payable is treated as "unused borrowing capacity," since delaying payments to suppliers is effectively borrowing from those suppliers. A quick check of his last bank statement reminded Jake that he had $160,000 left on his line of credit, which he had negotiated last year. This puts his total "unused borrowing capacity" at $177,000. With the $15,275 starting cash before checks were issued on 1-02-91, Jake was finally able to calculate Superdisk's cash capability (Table 1–3).

Jake continued to look elsewhere for cash. Picking up a copy of his latest financial statement (not illustrated), Jake read that Superdisk's total inventory was $925,900 and that accounts receivable were $813,456. The combination of these two accounts

TABLE 1–3

Cash Capability Calculation

Unused borrowing capacity	17,000
Unused bank line borrowing capacity	160,000
Cash in checking account	15,275
Cash Capability	$192,275

($1,739,356) represented a mine of potential cash that could be converted into actual cash to increase cash capability. Jake understood that squeezing these two accounts was an emergency measure. If he pushed too hard and long on accounts receivable, he would begin to lose customers. If he offered deep discounts on accounts receivable for too long, he would seriously impair Superdisk's profitability. If he reduced inventory below the proper amount, Superdisk would suffer stock outs and lose sales to competitors. For now, none of that mattered. Jake had to control a cash crisis and prevent it from becoming a meltdown, or lose his company. He began by requesting a current accounts receivable aging report from Joan.

Accounts Receivable Analysis

The accounts receivable aging report (Table 1–4) shows what is owed to Superdisk, Inc. for what length of time. Jake recognizes that there are many variables that must be coordinated. How close is inventory to shipment? Has anything else been shipped since the last accounts receivable aging report was produced? The completed cash budget will now help coordinate many of these variables. Let's look over Jake's shoulder as he studies Superdisk's 12-9-90 accounts receivable aging (Table 1-4). (The month-old date on the report reminds Jake of how answering a constant stream of vendor calls has put his normally prompt accounting department far behind in producing critical management reports.)

ABC is normal except for a $6,440.20 invoice. Joan tells him

TABLE 1–4

Accounts Receivable Aging Report
12-09-90 Posting

Customer	Current	30–60	61–90	Over 90	Total
ABC	52,845.65				
		6,440.20			59,285.85
Danborough	629,112.25				629,112.25
Flettner Drives				4,949.75	4,949.75
Hobart Moxness	2,932.80				
	7,329.40				
	64,320.10				
				1,442.35	76,024.65
Wisconsin Salami	2,338.05				
	5,669.95				8,008.00
Subatu, Inc.			36,075.00		36,075.00
Total	764,547.20	6,440.20	36,075.00	6,392.10	813,455.50

that there is a dispute over who should pay the shipping charge. Jake decides to pay the freight charge this time, in order to collect. Since the Danborough payment is critical to covering the float of the Vanadium Supply check, Jake calls Danborough and arranges to have their payment wired to Superdisk's checking account on the 9th.

Joan doesn't know why the Flettner Drives account is so overdue, so Jake calls Flettner's accounts payable department. He is eventually transferred to George Bianco, president of Flettner Drives, who tells him about his own cash problems. Jake has Joan put Flettner on "credit hold" and he makes an appointment to visit George Bianco that afternoon.

The Hobart Moxness "over 90" invoice for $1,442.35 looks

suspiciously like another disputed amount, but since it is too small to take his time, he directs Joan to follow up and collect it. (Once again, Jake makes a note of his accounting instructions so he will be able to follow up on even the smaller details related to cash.) The Wisconsin Salami receivables are current, so there is no "cash" to be found there.

Subatu has always been a reliable but slow account since it is overseas. Jake has his secretary telex Subatu, requesting payment by wire for the amount due. A return telex says that they will immediately wire funds to his account (recall that Jake floated two checks against this "certain" payment).

From the wire transfer, ABC's promise to pay, and the amount he expects to collect this afternoon from Flettner Drives, Jake has accumulated $47,464.95 ($36,075 + $6,440.20 + $4,949.75) to add to his cash capability of $192,275 (see Table 1-3). The total $239,740 is still not enough to take care of the big $382,785 bill due Rainbow Coatings, but it gives him some room to negotiate. In addition, Jake has arranged for the Danborough payment on the day the funds are due. Between the $239,740 and the Danborough receivable of $629,112, Jake will have $868,852—enough to finish paying off Rainbow Coatings' oldest billing for $382,785 and still make his $291,200 (224,000 + 67,200) payroll and payroll tax.

Next Jake calls Rainbow Coatings, calms down the boss, and explains that his cash is tied up in an abnormally large receivable, which he expects to collect in three days. His offer to send $195,000 now (from his cash capacity of $239,740) and the remainder in four days is accepted, and Superdisk has sufficient cash ahead for the next three weeks. Jake recorded the result of each of these negotiations on the emergency cash budget (Table 1-2).

For many small businesses, these types of emergency cash control measures constitute the full extent of cash planning, and they repeat the cycle until accounts payable borrowing capacity melts down, at which point they are tempted to use FICA or withholding taxes as a source of funds. *Borrowing from FICA and employee wage withholding taxes usually indicates imminent failure unless the company is able to find some additional investment money immediately.*

What Jake just did was to regain rudimentary control of his cash. Further emergency measures will be required before he begins the turnaround. The actual turnaround requires a great deal of analysis and usually several quarters to accomplish in a small company. Without further emergency measures, primarily layoffs, Jake would be doomed to repeat the initial cash control maneuvers until he finally ran out of room.

Before examining Superdisk's turnaround further, let's follow Jake to his afternoon appointment with George Bianco at Flettner Drives, which has suffered a total credit meltdown.

Recovering from a Credit Meltdown

Since Flettner Drives owes Superdisk $4,949.75, and because Jake is counting on Flettner's payment as part of Superdisk's cash capability, Jake has decided to pay George a personal visit, to see if he can save a customer. Jake finds George sitting in his office with a consultant's proposal on his desk. George says that he managed Flettner's unsolved cash-flow crisis for nearly a year before they had a meltdown of vendor credit.

The distinguishing feature of a meltdown is that further credit is refused and legal action is threatened or initiated to collect amounts owed. Another feature of a meltdown is that it feeds on itself: as credit is withdrawn, less cash is available to service accounts still extending credit, until they also withdraw credit. Finally, a meltdown happens quickly (in days or weeks) and often before management realizes that it is indeed a meltdown, rather than a series of unrelated credit withdrawals.

George couldn't believe how fast his cash disappeared once vendor credit was gone. Not knowing how to get Flettner Drives going again, George called a consultant, who left an outline for a recovery program. Recovery following a meltdown requires a dif-

16

ferent strategy than if a meltdown has not yet occurred. George invites Jake to read the proposal while he finds a way to clear up the obligation with Superdisk. Jake accepts and begins to read the consultant's program for handling a meltdown:

Credit Recovery Program for Flettner Drives

The record number of small business bankruptcies in the past decade gives mute testimony to the fact that many small businesses simply quit and seek bankruptcy protection when a meltdown of vendor credits exhausts their cash capability. This is unfortunate for two reasons. First, more often than not, they could have turned their company around even after a meltdown. Second, many of these small business people don't fully appreciate how serious bankruptcy can be—particularly if they want to start a new business because running their own business is what they are best suited to do. Bankruptcy can't always be avoided, but it should be viewed as a serious and negative consequence of business failure, and not an easy way out.

In a meltdown situation, the company loses credibility. Believability must be reestablished before credit can be regained. In a meltdown, the good news is that the worst has happened—the only direction, other than bankruptcy, is upward into better times.

Here is a checklist for recovery after meltdown:

1. As is always the case, honesty is the best policy in dealing with vendors after a meltdown. Generally, they are sympathetic and helpful if they understand that the company is trying to work out a turnaround, rather than go bankrupt.

2. Try to treat all vendors in an evenhanded fashion. Naturally, the ones who will work with the company will be trying to obtain most favorable treatment. Establish a policy for payment which treats all equally.

3. If there is not enough cash to pay all vendors a reasonably equal amount, then sort vendors according to how critical they are. The critical vendors are those who are single sources, major suppliers (large dollar volume of credit when normal relations are reestab-

17

lished), sources that give the company superior quality or price, and vendors that are company credit references.

4. Send a small partial payment on account. Resist setting up a payment schedule with some vendors until all vendors can be included in the plan. *You* must be in charge of payments, not your vendors.

5. Offer an incentive for trading old debt for new. In this case ask for new credit to be extended as old credit is retired. In many cases the company will be able to exchange dollar for dollar, but even cents on a dollar is significant.

6. Keep a running list of all the payment promises that have been made. Always meet these promises, or call back and let the vendor know that the company is still struggling. Don't ever fail to keep a promise, no matter how small, if it can be helped. If the company can't help it, always call and reestablish a new target. This is very hard for most people to do, so they tend to try to ignore the problem. Muster up your courage and call. If the vendor becomes abusive, tell him that it's hard enough to call, without being abused. This will usually calm down most people, when they think it through. Keep lines of communication open. Use the Golden Rule.

7. Don't let vendors know who other company vendors are. A group of three vendors can associate and push the company into involuntary bankruptcy. Generally, this is not seen by vendors as a good idea economically since they will receive only pennies on a dollar and only after a long time, but it is often used as a threat in order to obtain preferential payment treatment. Continue to make only partial payments even to those vendors who are threatening the company with legal action. Legal action is expensive and does not have a very high yield when dealing with small businesses. It is being used as a threat to win preferential treatment. Generally, a partial payment will quiet this type of threat.

8. *As a last resort,* offer to set up payment schedules. This is a formal arrangement rather than informally sending partial payments as suggested in point 4 above. Make certain to treat all vendors equally. Don't offer to pay one vendor in eight weeks and take twelve months to pay off another. Give the company as much time as you can negotiate. Extra time is extra cash. Explain that you need a

six-week moratorium to gather cash to begin making payments. Divide the payments into ten or twelve equal parts. Then do everything in the company's power to make certain that it doesn't miss a payment. If you offer to establish a payment plan, especially if in writing, always make certain that the terms are contingent upon written agreement of the vendor to extend credit on the basis of the new terms. Before sending out an offer to schedule out payments, contact a lawyer to make certain that the company offer is written correctly.

9. Try to obtain fresh credit from new vendors. They will want credit references, and if the company has kept its credit good with its credit references, then it may be surprising how easy it is to obtain new credit.

Remember, every time old debt is traded for new, or credit reestablished by paying off an account, or a new account opened with fresh credit, the company is increasing its cash capability and is a step closer to being able to plan for a turnaround.

The worse the cash crisis, the more closely it must be managed. It may be asked, just how bad is the cash crisis at this company? Subjectively, the problem of not being able to pay bills on time is viewed by different people in different ways. Some business people worry themselves to death if they are a week late with a vendor, while others go blithely forward into a cash crisis that threatens the viability of their company. There are, however, some objective measures: uncontested bills past due by 90 days or more and vendors' withdrawing credit, or threatening to, are two danger signs. Meltdown is defined as occurring when all credit is withdrawn. Obviously, anything short of meltdown is less serious than meltdown.

After meltdown, there are four major ways to go out of business:

1. Failure to pay FICA, federal, and state withholding tax.
2. Inability to purchase raw materials or make payroll.
3. Involuntary bankruptcy.
4. Giving up.

These are the "Big Four"—the really critical problems. If the company finds that it is flirting with any of them, it is in as much trouble as it can be.

No matter how difficult cash flow gets, always pay federal and state withholding taxes and FICA. This money does not belong to the company. The company collected it from its employees. To collect the taxes due, the tax authorities will come after management's personal assets and those of the directors of the company.

If a company is flirting with any of the "Big Four" problems, then cash management will become its central management chore until the problems have been resolved. In these dire circumstances, there are additional cash management activities in accounts receivable and banking that should be done. On the accounts receivable side, the company should be calling and offering incentives to receive early payment of its invoices. While these will eat into profits and have a long-term negative effect on cash, the long term does not apply when a company can't meet payroll or when it can't purchase the raw materials to keep the production line going.

The company should also be managing its float. Generally, there will be a period of time from when checks are mailed until they hit the account. Calculate float very carefully and keep daily watch on account balances at the bank. Banks catch on pretty quickly that a company is doing this and they don't like it. But, as long as the company doesn't overdraft its account, there is little that they are able to do to stop a company from using its float this way.

One word of caution: Don't float payroll. Payroll checks are local and they can be cashed directly at the company's bank. Bounced payroll checks have negative morale effects upon employees that are far greater than the effect of bounced vendor checks.

Beyond these special emergency measures, the cash control measures for meltdown companies are the same as those for companies that have not experienced a deep cash crisis.

George returned to the office cheered somewhat by the fact that Flettner could squeeze out a check for $4,949.75 to pay off Superdisk. Jake put the report down, thanked George, and returned to Superdisk more convinced than ever to turn around his company.

The Law of Cash Survival: Shrink, Don't Grow

The next morning when Jake returned to work, he decided to tackle a problem that he had been avoiding for a number of months. He had been hoping that Superdisk could "grow" its way out of the deepening cash crisis and that it would then be able to afford the personnel staffing level that had crept up over the years. The cash never appeared; in fact, it seemed to evaporate whenever he pushed to "grow into" the overhead structure of the company. Jake didn't like the idea of cutting back, but he realized that he didn't have much choice if he was running out of cash to make the payroll.

The iron law of cash survival is this: *A company cannot grow its way out of a cash crisis, but it can shrink its way out of it.* The CEO is going to have to reduce the size of the company to regain control of cash. This means reducing the number of people working at the company. A company cannot grow its way out of a cash crisis. Quite the opposite. More growth will place more strain on cash. If a company does not shrink its size as part of its emergency cash plan, it risks entering a downward spiral no matter how carefully its cash is managed.

Significant expense reduction always means payroll reduction. Whenever Jake has proposed a personnel reduction in the past, he heard a lot of arguments about why people couldn't be cut without damage to the company. He knew he would have to ignore arguments that the money could be saved by cutting back on travel or entertainment or any of the myriad "thrifty" ways to conserve cash without reducing personnel. It's true that every nonessential expense should be reduced before cutting people, because cutting good people cuts capacity. But Jake believed that careful trimming could leave capacity nearly the same at a much lower overhead rate, so he began to formulate his cut list.

The CEO Decides Who to Cut

A CEO should not ask his managers or department heads to produce a list of people to let go. In a small company asking for a "hit list" can ruin teamwork. The CEO must produce the list himself.

Malcontents and unmotivated employees obviously are at the

top of the list. Letting them go will provide cash without harming the productivity of the remaining people.

In order to help identify the deadwood, Jake looked at vacation and sick leave accruals. Those people who had used up most of their leave may not be pulling their weight. Since he always listened carefully, he knew who the sluggards and gossips were in Superdisk. The reduction in force would be the time to part ways with them.

If a manager argued too loudly and long against the cuts in his department, Jake would have to let him or her go, too. A cash flow crisis is no time to allow a "loyal opposition." If Jake was going to make a mistake in staff cuts for emergency cash control, he would make it in the direction of cutting too deeply. Otherwise he might have to do it again, and Jake knew multiple layoffs would discourage his remaining employees.

Although the cash effect of personnel cuts is rapid and very significant, they won't show up until the last week of Jake's emergency cash plan. The initial effect of paying accrued leave would create negative cash flow for the first pay period, but four weeks later the cash released by the cuts will become very significant.

Jake held onto his layoff list until he was ready to announce his "new operating plan" to the company as a whole. You'll see how he handled it later in the chapter.

Use Incentives During a Cutback

Jake knew that some of his best people were thinking of leaving, and he was aware that the best people leave first when opportunity fades. He sometimes thought of his company's struggle to survive as a war, and he knew that now was the time for battlefield promotions. It was time to help the malcontents out the door and to promote the producers.

Who were his best people—the real driving force behind the positive things that Superdisk had achieved? His first step was to identify who the winners were, recognizing their legitimate complaints but seeing the true pluses as well. By looking at the positive accomplishments of Superdisk and the people responsible for them, Jake was able to overcome some of his negative thoughts that stemmed from the cash crisis.

Having identified the best performers, it was Jake's job to reward them. An experienced manager, Jake knew the danger of promoting people to management positions who had no managerial experience. Managers must be trained before they can successfully assume the task of directing group efforts toward a company objective.

Since no excess cash is immediately available, management promotions were to be accompanied for now with very modest pay increases, but with a promise for more when Superdisk regains its normal posture.

Put Vacations and Perks on Hold

Jake understood that this was also the time to put a 90-day hold on all vacations. He wasn't afraid to promote or to promise a raise in the near future, but he had to make sure that the remaining cream of the crop would be coming to work over the next several months when his staff was leaner than normal. Since Jake was gathering strength for a turnaround, he knew he would need his key people on the front line with him. After the cash situation was stablized, Jake planned to reward those who helped during the crisis. But, for the duration of the cash crisis, he wanted every employee hour available to count.

Needless to say, Jake put all perks on hold, too, particularly his own. It would be impossible to ask an employee to forego a vacation if he saw the boss spending company money on a fancy car or club memberships. He also put a stop to the personal use of long distance telephone service, copy machines, and office supplies. Those items didn't add up to a great deal of cash saving, but they would send a strong signal that times were tough and that he meant business.

Mining Inventory for Cash

Inventory is a gold mine for intermediate term cash. Jake knew that there were two ways to control inventory to provide cash in 30 to 45 days during a cash flow crisis: stopping purchases and selling finished goods. Normally, his manufacturing manager controlled stock to make certain that he could make shipments on time. He kept his machines and manufacturing staff busy, so that he could purchase and produce in economic quantities. Jake knew that manufacturing was like a business within the business, and that he would have to get manufacturing in line with his corporate plan in order to succeed.

After assuring his manufacturing manager that this reduction of his spending authority was temporary, Jake made it a requirement that his signature be on all purchase orders. He reviewed the inventory for items that could be quickly moved out the door. As with his accountant, Jake needed the manufacturing manager to work very closely with him during the turnaround, and he needed a detailed understanding of the shape of inventory.

Jake asked for a sort of Superdisk's inventory by age. Using his best instinctive judgment, he drew a line separating the slow movers from the rest of his inventory. The slow movers would be put up for a "fire sale" to liquidate them for some cash.

Remembering that he was taking emergency measures, Jake knew that a great deal of analysis was neither possible nor required. He was looking for cash for survival, not maximum profitability right now.

Slow movers in inventory had already proven themselves to be less valuable than originally planned because they had been sitting uselessly, making Superdisk appear to have more assets than it really did. Many of them would have been written off during a physical goods inventory. Right now Superdisk needed cash, so Jake cleaned out the corporate attic and passed the savings along to his customers as a sales promotion.

Partial Shipments Generate Cash

Ship and invoice partial orders whenever customers will allow it. This is another way of mining inventory for cash. Most of Superdisk's customers were indifferent to partials, and some of them were quite pleased. Companies that are in cash trouble often have trouble shipping on time, and Superdisk was no exception. Partial shipments would help their cash position and improve relations with customers at the same time.

Unused Materials Are Sources of Cash

Return old unused materials for credit. This can be a particularly effective way of cleaning up accounts payable problems with key accounts. Jake requested a list of raw materials on hand by age and asked purchasing to return unneeded materials for credit. Even minus a hefty restock charge, dead materials were a cash resource with a double impact. Remember the problem with finding the cash to pay Rainbow Coatings $382,785? On his materials list, Jake found three barrels of Rainbow Coating Formula 99 that had been sitting in inventory for five months. His manufacturing manager told him that an order that used Formula 99 had been cancelled and the marketing forecast was wrong, so stock purchased per the forecast was still in the warehouse. So what if there was a 15% restock charge? This might be negotiated down in Superdisk's slow pay position, and Jake assumed that Rainbow Coatings wanted to keep Jake as a customer. Those three barrels were worth $189,000. Added to other sources of cash, a return of those unused materials could save an important source of credit from melting down.

Old materials that can't be returned for credit or somehow used in manufacturing should be sold for scrap. Since Superdisk routinely collected and sold scrap from its manufacturing process, Jake called in the junkman. Before the junkman arrived Jake asked his manufacturing manager and chief engineer if any of the material could be used in place of what was specified in Superdisk manufacturing processes. Sometimes a part number changed by engineering resulted in a pile of dead inventory when it was perfectly fit for use. Taking a tour of the stockroom and physically looking at the items to be scrapped helped manufacturing and engineering to see how they could be reclassified and used in place of another part that would otherwise have to be purchased at full expense.

Order Limited Quantities

Jake had to forego 'economic order quantities' (EOQ) during a cash crisis. (Manufacturing throughput concepts are discussed in detail in chapter two.) He purchased only what was necessary to fill existing orders. Superdisk's manufacturing and purchasing departments had developed a list of economic order quantities for certain materials and supplies. You can imagine Jake's frustration when he found that Superdisk had just been invoiced for a huge "once-every-two-years" automatic stock order for an EOQ of nuts and bolts when he only needed a fraction of that amount for the next month's shipments. Sure, it may cost Superdisk half again as much to order a month's supply at the regular rate ($19,500 instead of $13,000), but by ordering EOQ the company was billed $312,000. Jake would never again let an EOQ stock order be placed when he was fighting to regain control of cash.

Use Overtime to Ship Early

Jake wasn't afraid to use overtime to turn work in process into invoiced shipments. Normally, manufacturing tried to match labor to the flow of production in such a way that overtime didn't have to be paid. In the cash crisis, Jake looked at his work in process to see if there was anything that could be speeded up and shipped early. This was part of the process of increasing "throughput" for profitability and cash flow that would become part of the strategic turnaround as well as an emergency cash measure.

Sales Incentives

Next, Jake called a meeting with his sales people and gave them special incentives to move more product and to move it quickly. It would do no good to speed up throughput using overtime if the production merely bloated finished goods. Jake wanted to turn inventory into sales more quickly. Sales had to understand the game plan and do its part.

In the meeting he discussed the current sales compensation plan, which was a mixture of salary and commission. Jake told the sales people frankly that Superdisk could not afford to raise their salary or commission across the board until the financial position of the company was improved, but that he was willing to give them an extra commission on a one-time basis for the next 90 days on any items that were currently in inventory, a type of "bounty hunter" reward to solve a one-time problem.

Jake let sales know that a firm order backlog was a great asset to Superdisk during a cash shortage and that as soon as the company was back on its feet it would attempt to make a normal investment in inventory so that Superdisk's customers could be serviced in a more timely manner. Jake understood what he was asking. While slowing delivery by decreasing inventory, he was asking his sales force to keep a firm backlog—a task which would challenge them to the maximum.

Let Your People Know

Jake had to coordinate and communicate his cash control plan with company managers and employees. Jake knew that a frequent error in turning around small companies was attempting to do it piecemeal, without letting employees and managers know what was being done. He had already let some of his key managers and the sales staff know what he was being doing, so soon everyone would know, if they didn't already, that Superdisk was having financial trouble. He knew that he had to tell his employees that the small business that employed them was subject to the ups and downs of the competitive market place.

To put a positive light on what must be done to survive, Jake decided to present the turnaround as a new operating plan rather than using the financial term "turnaround." Jake's unveiling of the new operating plan would not emphasize the emergency nature of cash requirements, since he knew this would upset employees who were not financially sophisticated. Most employees would be looking for strong signs and new directions rather than an analysis of why one financial activity or another was being planned.

Handling Layoffs

Having already produced his layoff list, which reduced Superdisk's payroll overhead by 15%, Jake was faced with the unpleasant task of implementing his decision. He was determined to handle the layoffs firmly, and as thoughtfully as possible. Since the layoff included a dozen employees, Jake decided to do it en masse at the end of a work day. He chose a Monday because it would allow them to file for unemployment insurance benefits and look for a new job during the work week. Jake prepared information telling the laid off employees how to apply for unemployment insurance, and he had his accounting department produce all final paychecks including accrued vacation and sick leave.

On Tuesday morning after the lay off, Jake called a company meeting in the production area, which was large enough to accommodate the remaining employees. In a brief ten-minute speech he laid out the new operating plan and told the Superdisk employees that if they all pulled together, the company would succeed.

At this point Jake knew he had the most difficult part of the cash crisis management behind him and he would have the attention and cooperation of the remaining employees as he moved forward into the turnaround.

Emergency Cash Control Is *Not* a Turnaround.

Jake knew not to confuse emergency cash planning with the analysis and tasks necessary to produce a turnaround. Jake had been told that the difference between Superdisk before and after emergency cash control activities could be quite dramatic, particularly since the company had been wracked by a lack of cash control for a number of months. Having taken the bull by the horns and exerted control where there was none before, he was justifiably proud, but he knew not to confuse emergency control with a turnaround. Why not? There were two primary reasons:

First, the underlying problem that caused Superdisk to fall into trouble was yet to be identified. Lack of cash is always a symptom of a deeper malady in the company, not the cause. Analysis had to be done before corrective turnaround action could be taken. Second, many of the emergency procedures taken to control cash could not be sustained because they were not profitable in the long run.

Having obtained cash breathing room at a great price, Jake was highly motivated to move directly to the turnaround.

C H A P T E R   2

Analyzing
What Went
Wrong
at Superdisk

In Chapter 2, you will follow Jake and a friend, Helena, a financial analyst, as they appraise five years of Superdisk financial history to determine what went wrong financially. What they learn from looking at five years of history will help them to discover where Superdisk is "bleeding" and allow them to immediately cut off the main causes of Superdisk's long-term cash drain that led to it's current cash crisis.

The financial illustrations have been simplified to a bare-bones level so that by punching a few numbers on your calculator you can reproduce the analyses. This chapter and the next were written with nonmathematical and nonaccounting readers in mind. Nevertheless, there is no satisfactory way to completely verbalize financial analysis and some numerical work is required. In fact, you will want to study the calculations to make full use of the book. Upon finishing the book you should be able to plan a turnaround for your company, although you might call upon a financial professional for help in interpreting financial statements and preparing a financial forecast from the elements of your plan.

Analyzing Replaces Reacting

After Jake had cleared off urgent business at Superdisk, he closed the office door and began to think about how to turn his company around. How often had he thought about taking time out to analyze problems? It was always on his list of New Year's resolutions. Now financial distress has forced him to elevate analytical time to a high priority, and it would consume much of his work day.

As he began his analysis, Jake came to a basic concept: Plans can't turn a company around by themselves. *People* turn a company around by understanding, supporting, and executing a plan. In Chapter 1, Jake had already identified his best people—those who had contributed most to Superdisk's success were those he wanted to offer incentives to so they would commit their full energies to the turnaround.

Jake's list of the performers at Superdisk included employees in every area and every skill classification. He identified the leaders among these performers, the ones looked up to by the other employees. They were the people that must understand and accept the plan because they would implement the turnaround. Jake had eight real leaders and performers, about 10% of his work force.

Jake realized that a good plan would rest upon careful analysis of what was wrong with Superdisk. He had some ideas, but he wanted an outside view to confirm or challenge his preconceived ideas. Jake decided to call Helena, a friend who was a financial analyst for another manufacturing company, and ask if she would do a little consulting work for him at Superdisk.

When Helena arrived later that afternoon the first thing she asked Jake to do was give her the last five years of annual financial reports. Helena took the five years of history and made a five-year income history (Table 2–1) and balance sheet history (Table 2–4).

Analysis of Historical Profit and Loss

Sales Returns

Starting with the income history, Jake showed Helena how he had reversed the sales slide that had begun in 1987. By 1989 he had normalized sales and shown a big increase in 1990, which had just closed. However, Helena noticed that it looked like sales returns were going up. Although returns were still less than 2% of sales, they had risen from 1.1% in 1986 to 1.9% in 1990 and, therefore, were up 73% over five years (see Table 2–1).

Helena told Jake that returns should always be accounted for even if they are not very significant in their numerical effect on the bottom line. Sales returns that increase over a number of years is a danger sign related to falling morale in manufacturing. Falling morale in manufacturing translates into higher cost of goods sold, lack of competitiveness, loss of profitability, and, in extreme cases, failure of the company. Sales returns, although of slight effect themselves, serve as an excellent barometer of how well manufacturing is doing its job.

Gross Margin Components

Helena continued on down the income statement and saw a problem with the decrease in gross margin from 38.9% of sales in 1986 to 32.1% in 1990. In itself this trend was worrisome, but what it was hiding could be minor or major depending upon how the price component compared to the cost component in the gross margin.

TABLE 2–1

Superdisk, Inc. Five-Year Income History

	1986	1987	1988	1989	1990
Gross sales	$3,225,100	$3,125,600	$3,080,600	$3,205,600	$4,899,300
Returns	$35,476	$37,507	$40,048	$54,495	$93,087
Net sales	$3,189,624	$3,088,093	$3,040,552	$3,151,105	$4,806,213
Cost of goods sold	$1,935,060	$1,909,973	$1,909,972	$2,019,528	$3,233,438
Gross margin	$1,254,564	$1,178,120	$1,130,580	$1,131,577	$1,572,776
Gross margin %	38.90%	37.69%	36.70%	35.30%	32.10%
Operating expenses					
General & admin	$341,861	$334,439	$341,947	$339,794	$421,340
Marketing & sales	$322,510	$343,816	$354,269	$355,822	$440,937
Engineering	$258,008	$250,048	$246,448	$256,448	$391,944
R&D	$129,004	$125,024	$308,060	$192,336	$195,972
Total	$1,051,383	$1,053,327	$1,250,724	$1,144,399	$1,450,193
Pre-tax P/L	$203,181	$124,793	($120,143)	($12,822)	$122,583
Taxes at 45%	$91,432	$56,157	$0	$0	$0
Profit (Loss)	$111,750	$68,636	($120,143)	($12,822)	$122,583

There are two factors influencing gross margin: sales price and cost of goods sold. They need to be separated out for correction if there is a problem in the cost of goods sold.

Helena showed Jake that he had to do a little bit of cost accounting to separate the components in the gross margin. Jake had resisted this in the past because it required a time-consuming unit-by-unit analysis, but Helena insisted that Superdisk was blind without knowing why its gross margin had declined. What Helena does in Table 2–2 is demonstrate, in a hypothetical example, how to dissect the two components of gross margin and how a gross margin number "hides" superior or inferior performance of price or cost per sale.

Case A is an example of normal prices and unit costs. In case B the gross margin is below normal, and since the unit cost is within historical bounds, there is a price problem. This is valuable information. Why is there a price problem? Is the sales effort falling down or is competition driving the price down? In case C the cost is out of historical bounds. Is the manufacturing equipment wearing out? Are the manufacturing people spending too much time with a new computerized planning system? Are materials going up? In case D a nominal gross margin of 40% hides a

TABLE 2–2

Unit Analysis of Gross Margin

Case	Unit Price	Unit Cost	Gross Margin	Gross Margin %
A	$50	$30	$20	40%
B	$45	$30	$15	33%
C	$50	$34	$16	32%
D	$55	$33	$22	40%
E	$40	$24	$16	40%

Assumptions: (1) Normal gross margin is 40%. (2) The identical product is sold in all five cases.

superior sales performance and a problem in manufacturing. In case E the reverse is true.

By looking at Helena's hypothetical unit breakdown of gross margin, Jake could see that the raw gross margin figure could look fine yet be hiding problems. In the case of Superdisk, gross margin was showing a negative trend, which had to be investigated. Jake knew that it had been a number of years since he had adjusted the price of his product. Since inflation had caused his competitors to raise their prices while Superdisk remained the same, Superdisk was "buying" business. Jake had assumed that the increase in sales had been the result of adding a new product in 1990. But part of the big sales spike was coming from underpricing, or buying the sales. That was why the addition of new manufacturing equipment purchased in 1989 and 1990 hadn't seemed to do much to the gross margin.

Identifying the Money Losers

Helena showed Jake that he was "flying blind" if he did not take the time and expense to do rudimentary cost accounting. An analysis by product type (Table 2–3) showed that some products had gross margins of less than the 30% breakeven level required for profitability.[1] On those products, Superdisk was losing money on every item shipped out the door.

Superdisk's problem stood out in sharp relief after the products were separated by gross margin contribution. The main product, the full-size disk, was being produced below breakeven profit levels for the company. Declining prices and rock-bottom cost for the full-size disk had led Jake to develop a new product, the half-size disk, in 1989 and 1990, but the problem lingered. Superdisk did not have enough of the market to set up an offshore plant to

---

1. Helena calculated the breakeven gross margin percent using the following logic. From Table 2–1 for 1990, if gross margin of $1,572,776 fell to $1,450,193, exactly covering total operating expenses, there would be no profit. So $1,450,193 is the minimum gross margin required to break even, and the breakeven gross margin expressed as percent of sales is $1,450,193 ÷ $4,899,300 gross sales = 0.30 or 30%.

TABLE 2–3

Gross Margin Contribution by Product Type

Product Type	Gross Margin	Sales	Gross Margin Contribution
Full-size disk	29.1%	$2,789,120	$811,634
Half-size disk	37.9%	$1,245,560	$472,067
Backup tape drive	36.6%	$455,730	$166,797
Supplies	49.7%	$123,890	$61,573
Cables & connectors	21.3%	$285,000	$60,705
Total		$4,899,300	$1,572,776*

*Notice the $1,572,776 gross margin corresponds to 1990 in Table 2–1.

reduce manufacturing costs further, although its larger competitors had done just that. Jake had added new computer-controlled machines for efficient production of full-size disks in 1990, but that had not been enough to become cost competitive. If he dropped the full-size disk altogether, Superdisk would have to shrink to one-half its current size, which would make it extremely vulnerable to any downturn in sales.

Jake realized that as the sales of the new half-size disk increased, the gross margin would begin to slip because of price pressure necessary to gain additional market share. Superdisk would make some improvement in decreasing manufacturing costs as a result of the learning curve on the new product, but it wouldn't be enough to offset the loss suffered from the full-size disk product.

What Helena and Jake had learned so far was (1) that there was a possible morale problem in manufacturing resulting in lower quality and greater returns, and (2) that Superdisk was losing a little money on every one of its full-size disks shipped, a product that represented half of the business.

In addition to the full-size disk, the cables and connectors were also a substantial loser for Superdisk (see Table 2–3). These had to be shipped with each drive and were also sold separately, $285,000 worth. The supplies were a real winner and those were simply resale items. Jake made a mental note to reevaluate getting an outside supplier for the cables and connectors when he got to the planning stage.

Analysis of Historical Balance Sheet

Increased R&D Expense

Helena was now ready to move on to the balance sheet history. (Table 2–4) She started with the retained earnings portion of equity because retained earnings on the balance sheet are accumulated at the end of each year from the profit or loss total on the income statement.

For easy reference, retained earnings and profits are compared in Table 2–5. The years 1988 and 1989 showed a decline in retained earnings as a result of the losses in those years (for example, in 1988, a loss of $120,143 caused retained earnings to be decreased by that amount from the prior year). The company lost money in 1988 and 1989 because Jake had to increase R&D to bring out the new half-size disk product. As seen in Table 2–6, the increase in R&D expense in those two years over the prior two years at a near-constant sales volume gave Helena an estimate of the amount invested in the development of the new product: $248,948[2] if all else was equal.

Helena remarked that an increase in R&D of that size should have been planned and not financed out of operations as Jake had done.

2. From Table 2–6 for 1988, a "normal" R&D expense of 4% of $3,080,600 gross sales is $123,224. The actual R&D expense for that year is $308,060, an excess of $184,836 above the calculated normal expenditure for R&D. Using a similar calculation, 1989 shows an excess R&D expense of $64,112. The total excess of the two years, $248,948, represents the amount of R&D above normal paid as an expense.

TABLE 2–4

Superdisk, Inc. Five-Year Balance Sheet History

	1986	1987	1988	1989	1990
Assets					
Cash	$36,115	$65,820	$48,961	$55,490	$8,693
Accounts receiveable	$398,703	$411,746	$430,745	$472,666	$801,036
Inventory	$487,215	$503,153	$526,370	$577,598	$929,922
Fixed assets	$600,000	$550,000	$500,000	$450,000	$550,000
Total Assets	$1,522,033	$1,530,719	$1,506,076	$1,555,753	$2,289,650
Liabilities					
Draw on line of credit	$50,000	$0	$100,000	$150,000	$200,000
Accounts payable	$322,510	$312,560	$308,060	$320,560	$881,874
Long-term debt	$250,000	$250,000	$250,000	$250,000	$250,000
Total Liabilities	$622,510	$562,560	$658,060	$720,560	$1,331,874
Equity					
Paid in stock	$500,000	$500,000	$500,000	$500,000	$500,000
Retained earnings	$399,523	$468,159	$348,016	$335,193	$457,776
Total Equity	$899,523	$968,159	$848,016	$835,193	$957,776
Total Liabilities & Equity	$1,522,033	$1,530,719	$1,506,076	$1,555,753	$2,289,650

TABLE 2–5

Profits and Retained Earnings

	1986	1987	1988	1989	1990
Profit (Loss)	$111,750	$68,636	($120,143)	($12,822)	$122,583
Retained earnings	$399,523	$468,159	$348,016	$335,193	$457,776

TABLE 2–6

R&D Expensing

	1986	1987	1988	1989	1990
Gross sales	$3,225,100	$3,125,600	$3,080,600	$3,205,600	$4,899,300
R&D	$119,004	$125,024	$308,060	$192,336	$195,972
R&D % sales	4%	4%	10%	6%	4%

Improper R&D Funding

In examining the balance sheet history to try to find where the cash had come from for the new product development, Helena saw the increased draw on the line of credit. (Table 2–7 reproduces the relevant data from the balance sheet history.) Payables as a percentage of cost of goods sold shows how vendor credit was being misused to finance inventory sold. The purpose of the $360,000 line of credit was to finance short-term trade needs, not to make strategic investments. Was it a coincidence that the draw on the credit line had increased to $200,000 by 1990? Of course not. It had been the easiest money to obtain, so it had been used first. Jake's mistake was a classic misuse of a short-term credit line. Long-term debt, or equity, should have been used to finance long-term investments.

What had happened after the credit line was used up in 1990? The next available source of cash had been used—unauthorized borrowing from Superdisk's suppliers. As can be seen in Table 2–7, 1990 accounts payable had increased dramatically from its histori-

TABLE 2–7

Expansion of Credit Line Drawings and Payables

	1986	1987	1988	1989	1990
Draw on credit line	$50,000	$0	$100,000	$150,000	$200,00C
Accounts payable	$322,510	$312,560	$308,060	$320,560	$881,874
Payables %					
Cost of goods sold	16.7	16.4	16.1	15.9	27.3

cal average. The historical average trade account was aged 60 days, but the average age of 1990 accounts translated into 98 days,[3] which placed the company at the edge of a supplier credit meltdown. Since most of A/P is composed of money owed for items that comprise the product at Superdisk, this aging figure gives a good yardstick to measure whether or not the company is misusing vendor credit. If there is a large labor component to cost of goods sold, then this method should not be used; in that case, compare payables to the materials component of costs of goods sold.

Thus the root cause of the accounts payable problems has been found: Short-term supplier credit had been used to finance new product development.

Banks won't loan for R&D because they are cash flow lenders, not venture capitalists. Jake knew very well that he couldn't go to the bank for a long-term loan with the two years of loss. He could explain that the loss was due to investment in a new product, but the bank was interested in evidence of cash flow to support additional lending, and cash flow increases from the new product were still many months in the future. Jake now realized that he should have made an equity offering or attempted to find a source of long-term debt *before* he embarked on developing a new product.

3. From Tables 2–1 and 2–4 for 1990: 360 days × $881,874 accounts payable ÷ $3,233,438 cost of goods sold = 98 days. Compare this with the historical 1986 average age: 360 days × $322,510 accounts payable ÷ $1,935,060 costs of goods sold = 60 days.

TABLE 2–8

Increased Investment in Inventory

	1986	1987	1988	1989	1990
Inventory	$487,215	$503,153	$526,370	$577,598	$929,922
Inventory % cost of goods sold	25.2	26.3	27.6	28.6	28.8

Cuts in Accounting Dammed Up Cash Flow

The analysis of the balance sheet history brought out some other trends that Jake would reverse in his planning. Accounts receivable had slowly moved upward from 45 to 59 days[4] over the five-year period. Cost accounting, which Jake had vetoed as an unnecessary expense, would have given Jake a good tool to judge the relative profitability of Superdisk products. As sales increased so did the load of paperwork in accounting, and they had to handle it with a smaller staff. As accounts payable went over 60 days, and particularly as they approached the meltdown level of 98 days, the accounting staff's time was spent dealing with putting off payments rather than collecting what was owed. That "little" addition of 14 days in the age of accounts receivable used $190,528 in cash, which otherwise would have been collected and available.[5]

Inventory Control Problems

Analysis of the balance sheet also revealed a problem in inventory control. The relevant data is reproduced in Table 2–8. As is evident in the Table, inventory as a percentage of cost of goods

4. From Tables 2–1 and 2–4 for 1990: 360 days × $801,036 accounts receivable ÷ $4,899,300 gross sales = 59 days. Compare with 1986: 360 days × $398,703 accounts receivable ÷ $3,225,100 gross sales = 45 days.
5. For 1990: 360 days × increased cost of receivables ÷ $4,899,300 gross sales = 14 days. Solving for the increased cost of receivables yields $190,528 of new receivable investment required.

sold had crept up over the last five years, tying up an additional $116,404[6] cash in excessive inventory.

Managing Current Assets to Regain Credit

Helena made a quick calculation that $341,890 was needed to pay down accounts payable to historical levels of 16.7% of cost of goods sold.[7] Jake could almost do this if he brought accounts receivable down by $190,528 and inventory down by $116,404 to 1986 proportions. This wouldn't solve the long-range profitability problems of Superdisk, but it would go a long way toward reducing the cash crisis and regaining credit with his suppliers and the bank.

Jake decided to dwell for a moment on profitability. He knew that firms in his industry earn 12% pre-tax profit on sales as an average. For Superdisk to attain this level, would require an improvement in gross margin from 32.1% (1990 gross margin) to 42%.[8] Improvements in the gross margin involves increasing prices, decreasing cost of goods sold, and rationalizing the existing product mix. Jake made a note of his profit goal and resolved to work to attain it over coming years as soon as Superdisk was beyond its cash crisis.

The day with Helena had gone by quickly. When Jake went home that evening he felt like he was really making progress. Far from being a disaster, he was beginning to see how Superdisk could be a real winner again.

6. From Table 2–8: (28.8% − 25.2% benchmark) × $3,233,438 cost of goods sold in 1990 = $116,404.

7. From Tables 2–1 and 2–4 for 1986: $322,510 accounts payable ÷ $1,935,060 cost of goods sold = 16.7%. For 1990, using the desired (historical) 16.7%: 0.167 × $3,233,438 cost of goods sold = $539,984. This is what the 1990 accounts payable ideally should be. The difference between desired and actual is $881,874 − $539,984 = $341,890 excess accounts payable.

8. From Tables 2–1 and 2–4 for 1990: 12% desired pre-tax profit × $4,899,300 gross sales = $587,916 desired 1990 profit. But actual profit was $122,583, which is a $465,333 shortfall. Assuming all profit improvement comes from gross margin, the target gross margin as percent of gross sales is: $1,572,776 gross margin + $465,333 desired increase in profit = $2,038,109 ÷ $4,899,300 gross sales = 42%.

Deepening the Analysis

The next morning Helena was back at Jake's office to finish the preliminary financial review. After they produced a summary of what they had found in the historical financials, the analysis could begin in earnest. Preliminary financial analysis of historical financial records merely points out the potential areas for improvement. Additional analysis often must be done in the problem areas to find out where the bleeding is and to form a plan of action to cope with it.

Jake summarized the preliminary findings in writing so that he could easily remember the information when they made detailed investigations of pricing, manufacturing, and inventory practices. His summary is shown in Table 2–9. The next stage of analysis will deal with determining where cost of goods sold can be decreased and where price can be increased within the existing operation. Remember, these are the two elements of gross margin that Jake has to work with to improve Superdisk's financial picture. This analysis will help to maximize profitability which, of course, is the long-term solution to cash flow problems once basic financial management discipline has been instituted.

Jake called in his marketing manager and asked her to probe the competition for pricing information. Although list prices were published, the computer disk marketplace demanded negotiation for major original equipment manufacturer (OEM) contracts. (An OEM is a manufacturer whose product is an important and standard part of a product sold by another company.) Jake knew the competitor's prices he would get for comparison would fall in a range of values and that no competitor's product was an exact equivalent of his own, either in features or perceived value. Even so, the information would provide a basis for evaluating price on Superdisk's main products.

Meanwhile he would investigate the cost of goods sold.

Jake went back to manufacturing and asked for a computer listing of inventory. He noted that a physical inventory had not been

TABLE 2–9

Historical Financial Analysis: Summary of Findings

1. Eight top employee performers have been identified.

2. Sales returns have crept up by 73% in five years. This indicates a possible morale problem in manufacturing reflecting itself in quality problems.

3. The old product line, particularly the full-size disk, has not been repriced for several years.

4. Cables and connectors are a small-volume product, but they are the worst loser, garnering only a 21.3% gross margin.

5. Cutbacks in accounting, coupled with increased demands in payables and a sales volume increase, has resulted in accounting being understaffed.

6. Undermanning in sales is being masked by an increase in total sales, while the new product is contributing less sales than planned. This is compounding the gross margin problem.

7. The new product has been financed by short-term credit, rather than through long-term debt or equity. This has soaked up the line of credit and stressed accounts payable to the point of near meltdown.

8. The required reduction in accounts payable of $341,890 will bring it back to a normal 60-day aging.

9. If accounts receivable could be reduced to 45 days, it would yield $190,528 cash.

10. Inventory should be reduced by $116,404 to historical best levels.

11. To get to a respectable pre-tax profit of 12%, gross margin must be increased from 32% to 42% over the next five years.

performed at the end of the last year due to the shortage of accounting people and the need for manufacturing to keep the wheels turning in their recent growth cycle. As he was working through the analysis, Jake was gaining an appreciation of how difficult it must be for his managers to make informed judgments with out-of-date and incomplete reports. An accurate inventory count and inventory cost is essential to knowing how much it costs to make the item sold. If cost of goods sold is merely estimated, as it was at Superdisk, then the amount by which inventory was received is incorrect and the profit or loss from that period is also incorrect. Soon, the monthly financial reports become entirely misleading.

Aim for Throughput, Not Economic Order Quantities

While his marketing and manufacturing managers gathered the price and inventory data he needed, Jake and Helena took a tour of the manufacturing floor. Manufacturing is the source of inventory quantity and cost data, which comprise the cost of goods sold. For Jake, giving a tour of manufacturing was one of the most satisfying parts of his job. Jake liked to see each machine running at optimum level, everything humming at the same time. What Jake did not realize is that a humming factory may be an inefficient factory.

Helena looked at manufacturing in a different way. She knew that company throughput efficiency is *not* a sum of departmental efficiencies. She suggested that Jake view manufacturing as a single machine that had to be optimized rather than as a series of individual machines to be run at optimum rate. What was the difference?

Helena explained that when the company was optimized as a single machine for "throughput," some parts would be idle. However, the productive parts of the company "machine" would be working for a profit rather than loading inventory with runs of "economic order" size in the hope of some future, yet unbooked, sales. *Throughput is a measure of manufacturing that considers the*

46

company as a single machine producing to booked orders rather than to economic order quantities. Production based on economic order quantities wastes cash, decreases throughput, and destroys profits.

This was an important distinction that goes against the grain of many manufacturing managers, particularly those schooled during World War II and in the 1950s and 1960s when the ideal was to keep the factory humming at all times. But World War II was a peculiar economic situation, one in which national survival took precedence over cost of production—hardly a model for efficient business, even though it dominated business education for the next two decades. Stated another way, World War II provided the equivalent of "booked orders" for anything that could be produced, a situation which lasted into the postwar period in the form of pent-up demand for housing and consumer goods of all types.

To model manufacturing in today's competitive environment upon manufacturing techniques of the 1940s and 1950s would result in piling up inventory and chewing up cash. Ultimately, significant portions of the inventory became obsolete, causing a loss.

Viewing the company as a single machine dedicated to producing *only firm booked orders* is the way to overcome the problem of "economic order quantity" thinking that became institutionalized in business education in the decades following the 1940s. The more throughput—actual booked orders—that can be produced with the same labor force and equipment per unit of time, the greater the profit for the company.

Managing Bottlenecks in Production

Manufacturing's preoccupation with optimal production runs—*i.e.,* holding up production of orders until large quantities of the same item could be run—helped explain why marketing often complained at company staff meetings that manufacturing was never able to keep its schedule of deliveries. These schedule slips caused a loss of customers over the long run.

Helena noted that parts to be processed were piled up behind several of the machines on the floor. Jake said he couldn't justify faster machines or a larger night shift, so they just worked with bottlenecks. Helena suspected that the piles of parts were evidence of the wasteful "optimum production run" type of thinking, and that even if he had faster equipment or more staff, those parts would still be sitting there.

Looking at the routing tickets, she asked Jake which of them were for current orders. Out of ten jobs, Jake found only one that was for inventory rather than shipment. But a closer look revealed that every job, except one rush order, was partly to meet a current order and partly to meet economic order quantities. In effect, producing economic order quantities to inventory was holding up booked orders at the bottlenecks.

Jake could often spot bottlenecks on the manufacturing floor simply by looking for piles of work in process or raw materials sitting beside a machine, particularly if there were several separate jobs in the queue. To improve throughput of the company, Jake now realized he must insist that machines and processes that were bottlenecks to the flow of throughput must be dedicated to the production of booked orders. Holding up orders to manufacture economic order quantities, thereby creating bottlenecks, was false economy. Such notions of "savings" increased the cost of goods sold, hurting gross margin.

Jake decided to direct his manufacturing managers to tag the jobs filling current customer orders with a colored routing, easily recognizable in the shop, and instruct them that their goal was to complete those jobs as quickly as possible.

Increasing Throughput Decreases Cost

By Helena's estimate, simply differentiating between customer orders and inventory orders and stopping the manufacture of economic order quantities at bottlenecks would reduce the cost of goods sold by 5%. Jake wanted to know how. Helena explained that if throughput is increased per unit of time without adding to the labor force, then the overhead contribution per unit of production is spread further. If additions to the labor force further increase throughput, as is possible, then they might also be economical. The key is watching profit. Machines should be turning to fill customer orders, not inventory shelves. Few companies, especially small ones, can or should increase their overhead to eliminate all bottlenecks. The key is to make certain that an immediately invoiceable product pours through those bottlenecks, rather than a product destined for inventory.

Deflating the Work-in-Process Balloon

When they returned to the office later that afternoon the inventory report was ready. What Helena had predicted was immediately evident in the large work-in-process portion of the inventory. A tour of the stock room confirmed Jake's suspicions about the accuracy of the routing report he had questioned earlier in the day. The shelves were full of "economic order" and "economic production batch" parts. Some of the parts were so old that they were beginning to rust. Only infrequently would an empty bin be found, and with it a routing slip showing that the shop had an order to produce more. By limiting bottlenecks to production of booked orders, Jake now had a rational tool for deflating the work-in-process balloon that had been devouring Superdisk's cash and reducing its profitability.

Spotting Inventory Orphans

The biggest surprise came in the cables and connectors storage area. Perhaps it was a big surprise to Jake because bringing cable and connector manufacturing in house had always been his pet project. There were dozens of shelves with neatly tagged bundles of cables and bins of custom connectors. A briefing from the stores clerk told the story. Almost every one of the customers had a different cabling requirement. Sometimes they changed their floor plan at the last minute and the cables would go into inventory because sales didn't want to lose the order by charging for a normally included "service" to the customer. Some of the cables had gone into inventory as the result of an attempt to standardize cable configurations so they could be shipped off the shelf. Some of the cables had become orphans when engineering made a minor change in the wiring of a product requiring a change in cables. Every customer return had left orphan cables that over the years had accumulated into a mountain of dead inventory.

Not only were the cables being made at a loss, as was revealed in the analysis of gross margin by product type, they were bulking up inventory, draining precious cash that could be used to save the company credit and later to apply to new product development and greater profit potential. Jake was not consoled by Helena's observation that *most companies requiring a turnaround had a "bleeder," and that the bleeder was often a pet project of the boss or a sacred cow.*

Jake had to wait a few days for marketing's price report so he couldn't get on with planning yet, but he knew enough to get rid of the cables. Starting immediately, customers would once again have to go to a cable supplier to cable their site. Sales estimated that loss of this service would cost the company 10% of its sales in the full-size disk, which was in an extremely defensive position already. Loss of cabling would have little effect on the new half-size disk, because demand for the product was so great. The net effect of abandoning the cable and connector line would be that Superdisk would lose sales, but that the gross margin on the remaining sales would improve and valuable cash would be freed.

Managing Price to Improve Gross Margin

When the pricing data came in later the next week, Jake got together with Helena once again to analyze it. Marketing estimated that the price of the full-size disk could be increased by

4% (up to the competition) without a noticeable drop in the order rate. An increase of 6% would cause a loss of 20% of sales of that product. The 6% increase in sales price would improve the gross margin by 3%. That was the good news. The bad news was that none of the other products could bear a price increase at all, and that the market for the full-size disk was going to disappear altogether in the next three years. Furthermore, it was expected that the current tight supply for the half-size disks would disappear in the next twelve months and that the price of the half-size disk would have to come down. Jake was kicking himself mentally for not aggressively grabbing market share during the early stages of the half-size disk life cycle.

Jake decided that he had little choice other than to begin to phase out the full-size disk. By raising prices 6% he would lose 20% of his volume, but the 3% improvement in gross margin would convert the main product from a bleeder into a slightly profitable product for a while. Jake realized that he had little time to put together a profit plan and that he would also have to begin planning a new product immediately.

The financial crisis at Superdisk placed Jake in a position where he had to think fast, act fast and begin planning ahead. Analysis of historical financials records and some cost accounting revealed that Superdisk had financed its R&D with short-term credit, a major mistake and the leading cause of near credit meltdown. Jake's analysis led him to to scrap some products and emphasize others. Finally, Jake learned that throughput was the correct measure of efficient production planning, not production to economic order quantities.

In the next chapter, Jake and Helena will take what they have learned by analyzing past performance of Superdisk and project it into the future as a forecast for the company.

Financial
Forecasting
for the
Post-Turnaround
Company

Having stopped the two main sources of bleeding—poor financial management and over production of inventory—Jake was now ready to make a five-year financial plan. The five-year financial forecast will look just like the five-year historical financial records that Jake and Helena analyzed in Chapter 2. They will forecast the future starting with a projection of Superdisk's current year ending 12-31-91. In Chapter 3, as you will watch as Jake and Helena work through the planning process, you will learn how to produce an integrated financial forecast. With this tool, you will not only be able to plan your company's future, but you will be able to run unlimited financial "what if" possibilities.

The Forecast Is Comprised of Three Documents

First Helena reviewed the flow of information in the forecast. She pointed out that although producing an integrated financial forecast was somewhat complex, there was no reason for it to thwart planning as it often does in a small company like Superdisk.

A. There are three documents that must be forecast: (1) profit and loss (or income statement) forecast; (2) balance sheet forecast; and (3) cash flow forecast. (See Tables 3–1, 3–2, and 3–3).

B. Generally, the income forecast is prepared first, then the balance sheet, then the cash flow forecast. The income forecast tells whether a company has made a profit or a loss during a defined period of time, which can be monthly, quarterly, year to date, or annually. The balance sheet is simply a statement of the net worth of the company at a point in time: assets minus liabilities equal net worth (also known as equity). Both the income statement and the balance sheet affect cash if conditions change. Therefore, the cash flow forecast cannot be made until the income statement and balance sheet forecasts are complete for the period.

C. Income, balance sheet, and cash flow are related by accounting techniques and the integration of financial information. The term "integrated" simply means that whatever is stated in one document must correspond to a dependent variable in another statement. A dependent variable is a result or condition that must change if the factor it depends upon is changed. For example, retained earnings on the balance sheet is an accumulation of prior profits and losses retained by the company. It depends upon profit or loss reported on the income statement. Notice in Table 3–1 that the 1995 profit of $360,391 constitutes the increase in retained earnings from $1,113,165 to $1,473,556.

D. Although the flow of information is usually from the income statement to the balance sheet to the cash flow statement, there are a few exceptions. For instance, company borrowing depends upon its cash needs, which are influenced by a multitude of variables. The interest on the loan for the period cannot be specified until the amount to be borrowed is known. The interest is reflected on the "other income (expense)" line of the income forecast, which changes profit, which changes cash available, which modifies the amount of interest paid. This sounds more complex at first than it is in practice.

E. Because assets must always equal liabilities plus equity, the

TABLE 3–1

Superdisk, Inc. Five-Year Income Forecast

	1991	1992	1993	1994	1995
Gross sales	$3,777,564	$3,530,056	$4,229,808	$4,860,160	$5,684,200
Returns	$60,000	$55,000	$50,000	$65,000	$70,000
Net sales	$3,717,564	$3,475,056	$4,179,808	$4,795,160	$5,614,200
Cost of goods sold	$2,280,000	$2,000,000	$2,400,000	$2,700,000	$3,110,000
Gross margin	$1,437,564	$1,475,056	$1,779,808	$2,095,160	$2,504,200
Gross margin %	38.06%	41.79%	42.08%	43.11%	44.06%
Operating expenses					
General & admin	$377,756	$353,006	$422,981	$486,016	$568,420
Marketing & sales	$377,756	$353,006	$422,981	$486,016	$568,420
Engineering	$302,205	$282,404	$338,385	$388,813	$454,736
R&D	$151,103	$141,202	$169,192	$194,406	$227,368
Total	$1,208,820	$1,129,618	$1,353,539	$1,555,251	$1,818,944
Other income(expense)	($54,000)	($39,600)	($43,800)	($36,600)	($30,000)
Pre-tax profit	$174,744	$305,838	$382,469	$503,309	$655,256
Taxes at 45%	$78,635	$137,627	$172,111	$226,489	$294,865
Profit(Loss)	$96,109	$168,211	$210,358	$276,820	$360,391

TABLE 3–2

Superdisk, Inc. Five-Year Balance Sheet Forecast

	1991	1992	1993	1994	1995
Assets					
Cash	$34,287	$35,344	$36,500	$41,182	$44,588
Accounts receiveable	$517,361	$483,612	$581,690	$667,326	$781,310
Inventory	$671,660	$590,036	$706,136	$795,673	$916,078
Fixed assets	$600,000	$700,000	$800,000	$900,000	$1,050,000
Total Assets	$1,823,308	$1,808,993	$2,124,326	$2,404,181	$2,791,976
Liabilities					
Draw on line of credit	$200,000	$80,000	$115,000	$55,000	$0
Accounts payable	$415,532	$353,006	$422,981	$486,016	$568,420
Long-term debt	$250,000	$250,000	$250,000	$250,000	$250,000
Total Liabilities	$865,532	$683,006	$787,981	$791,016	$818,420
Equity					
Paid in stock	$500,000	$500,000	$500,000	$500,000	$500,000
Retained earnings	$457,776	$625,987	$836,345	$1,113,165	$1,473,556
Total Equity	$957,776	$1,125,987	$1,336,345	$1,613,165	$1,973,556
Total Liabilities & Equity	$1,823,308	$1,808,993	$2,124,326	$2,404,181	$2,791,976

TABLE 3–3

Superdisk, Inc. Five-Year Cash Flow Forecast

	1991*	1992	1993	1994	1995
Beginning cash	$0	$34,287	$35,344	$36,500	$41,182
Gross profit (loss)	$0	$345,438	$426,269	$539,909	$685,256
(Interest expense)	$0	($39,600)	($43,800)	($36,600)	($30,000)
(Tax expense)	$0	($137,627)	($172,111)	($226,489)	($294,865)
(Increase)Decrease to accounts receivable	$0	$33,749	($98,078)	($85,636)	($113,983)
(Increase)Decrease to inventory	$0	$81,623	($116,100)	($89,536)	($120,405)
(Increase)Decrease to fixed assets	$0	($100,000)	($100,000)	($100,000)	($150,000)
Increase(Decrease) to draw on line of credit	$0	($120,000)	$35,000	($60,000)	($55,000)
Increase(Decrease) to accounts payable	$0	($62,526)	$69,976	$63,034	$82,404
Increase(Decrease) to long-term debt	$0	$0	$0	$0	$0
Increase(Decrease) to paid in stock	$0	$0	$0	$0	$0
Ending Cash	$34,287	$35,344	$36,500	$41,182	$44,588

*Since a cash flow is a record of relative change, the initial values are $0.

balance sheet can be forced to "solve for cash." This means that the figure in the "cash" line on the balance sheet is the result of the interaction of all the variables on the income statement and the balance sheet. This allows great flexibility in testing business alternatives quickly, without constructing a detailed cash flow. By manipulating all other variables and solving for cash, Jake can do an infinite number of "what if's" with the other variables and note what happens to cash.

What happens to cash is of supreme importance to financial management, particularly if low or negative cash is predicted. The trick of forcing cash rather than producing a detailed cash flow statement is a tremendous shortcut to planning, particularly if using a computer spreadsheet. (After spending a few hours with a computer spreadsheet, you will be utterly convinced of the financial merits and potential of business planning with a computer.)

Isn't computing cash the function of the cash flow statement? Partially. The "forced cash" line in an integrated balance sheet will always equal the equivalent "ending cash" line in the cash flow statement for the same period, but it does not give all the rich detail the cash flow statement does. Ideally, the cash flow statement will give enough detail that those using it can see what is using cash and what is producing cash in the company.

Formatting the Financial Statements

Preparing an integrated financial forecast involves formatting the documents and producing the equations that calculate or display each line of the documents. Some lines are calculated, some lines are filled in with data. Forecasts can be produced on paper spreadsheets the old-fashioned way or on computer spreadsheets, whichever is available.

Since there will be three distinct documents, Jake needed to set up three separate spreadsheets for the statements: Income (profit and loss), balance sheet, and cash flow. In order to make the financial plan easy to read, Helena suggested that it be forecast on an annual basis. Most investors like to see the first year spread out by months, the second two years by quarters, and the last two years annually, but to learn the planning method, annual periods work best since they are easy to comprehend on a single page.

Income Statement Format

Although there are no fixed rules for what categories can appear in an income statement, Helena reminded Jake that there are very firm rules about how the various segments of the statement relate to each other and what type of information flows into each of the segments. Jake asked Helena to lay out the basic elements of an income statement for Superdisk. She produced the following list of line items (these are identical to the line items that appeared in the historical income statement she prepared for Jake in Chapter 2):

Line Item	How the Information Gets There
Gross sales	Numerical estimate by Jake, to be derived from unit volume and price forecasts.
Returns	Numerical estimate by Jake, based upon past experience.
Net Sales	Calculated: Gross sales minus returns.
Cost of goods sold	Numerical estimate by Jake. Cost of goods sold are manufacturing costs before any administrative, marketing, or R&D expenses are deducted. A practical way of obtaining this is to take last year's cost of goods sold as a percentage of sales and adjust it for any known increases or decreases in cost of manufacture.

Gross margin	Calculated: Net sales minus cost of goods sold.
Gross margin %	Calculated: Gross margin as a percent of gross sales.
Operating expenses	Category heading used to group expenses.
General and Administrative	Calculated: 0.1 times gross sales is the amount Jake decided to budget, based upon past experience.
Marketing and sales	Calculated: 0.1 times gross sales is the amount Jake decided to budget, based on past experience.
Engineering	Calculated: 0.08 times gross sales is the amount Jake decided to budget, given past experience.
R&D	Calculated: 0.04 times gross sales is the amount Jake decided to budget, given past experience.
Total operating expense	Calculated: Sum of operating expense categories.
Other income (expense)	Calculated: Interest expense on debt for the period. The first step is to find the amount of debt for the period in the balance sheet categories "draw on line of credit" and "long-term debt" (see balance sheet, Table 3–2). At Superdisk both loans bear a 12% rate. As an example for 1991, ($54,000) = 12% × ($200,000 + $250,000).
Pre-tax profit	Calculated: Gross margin minus total operating expense minus other expense or plus other income.

Taxes at 45%   Calculated: 0.45 times pre-tax profit.

Profit (Loss)   Calculated: Pre-tax profit minus taxes.

Balance Sheet Format

Having completed the income forecast, Helena began to set up the balance sheet for Superdisk. She cautioned Jake that the historical ratios between variables observed at Superdisk would not necessarily hold true in the future, and that they were quite different from those observed in service companies; for instance, a service company may have a much larger relative advertising budget and smaller inventory than a manufacturing company. Every company has its own financial "fingerprint" that describes a healthy relationship among financial variables. Helena told Jake that he must continually measure the relationship established between the income forecast and the balance sheet forecast because they were likely to change, and that any forecast was better when it was frequently tested and updated.

Helena started at the bottom segment of the balance sheet and worked her way upward since her objective was to force the balance sheet to "solve for cash."

Line Item	*How the Information Gets There*
Equity	Category heading used to group net worth items.
Paid in stock	Numerical estimate by Jake. This is the sum of all money paid for stock in the history of the company to that point in the forecast.
Retained earnings	Calculated: Sum of prior year's retained earnings and current year's profit or loss.

Total equity	Calculated: sum of retained earnings and paid in stock.
Liabilities	Category heading.
Draw on line of credit	Numerical estimate by Jake. Once the integrated forecasts are complete and able to solve for cash, Jake will vary the draw on line of credit to "tune" the plan to just enough cash, but not more than needed. Almost no one wants to hold excessive cash because almost all companies are paying interest on borrowed funds.
Accounts payable	Calculated: For the first year 0.11 times annual gross sales is used because the line of credit remains exhausted. From 1992 on, the budgeted amount is 0.1 times gross sales (annual). This relationship has been observed in Superdisk history and is projected to remain. Other companies may wish to tie accounts payable to the cost of inventory production and operating expense instead.
Long-term debt	Numerical estimate by Jake.
Total liabilities	Calculated: Sum of draw on line of credit, accounts payable, and long-term debt.
Total liabilities and equity	Calculated: Sum of total liabilities and total equity.
Assets	Category heading.
Total assets	Calculated: Set equal to total liabilities and equity as required by the basic accounting equation.

Accounts receivable   Calculated: net sales ÷ 12 × 1.67. (The 1.67 multiplier yields 50 days receivable.)

Inventory   Calculated: (net sales ÷ 12) × (1-gross margin %) × 3.5. (1 − gross margin % yields the cost of goods sold multiplier which, when multiplied by monthly sales, yields cost of goods sold for an average month).

Fixed assets   Numerical estimate by Jake. This is based upon the value of existing and new equipment purchased to produce enough to meet the sales forecast. Superdisk adds about $100,000 of equipment each year.

Cash   Calculated: Total assets minus accounts receivable minus inventory minus fixed assets.

As an example, let's follow Jake's calculation for cash for 1992. The figures are from Table 3–2. In order to obtain ending cash, Jake starts by calculating the *prior* year's cash as a percentage of gross sales: $34,287 ÷ $3,777,564 = 0.0091. For 1992, estimated cash is then 0.0091 × $3,530,056 gross sales = $32,040. Next he totals all 1992 assets: $32,040 + $483,612 + $590,036 + $700,000 = $1,805,688, which is a temporary total assets. By definition assets must equal liabilities plus equity. So Jake subtracts from the temporary total assets all liabilities and equity, *excluding the credit line draw* (remember, Jake will vary this draw to "tune" his forecast): $1,805,688 total assets − $1,125,987 equity − $603,006 liabilities excluding credit = $76,695. This is the credit needed to make assets equal to liabilities plus equity. Since credit must be drawn in increments of $5,000, the credit draw becomes $80,000, not $76,695. The difference of $3,304 is added to cash to produce $35,344, final cash.

Cash Flow Format

Jake thought everything was pretty clear so far, but he asked why it was necessary to make a cash flow forecast since the balance sheet forecast already solved for cash. Helena explained that while the cash line in the balance sheet forecast would always equal the ending cash on the cash flow forecast, the cash flow forecast would, in addition, make visible the separate factors affecting ending cash for the period. With the cash flow forecast, Jake would be able to see which financial variables were important during the period and which ones weren't.

Since a cash flow statement shows the calculated changes in cash relative to a prior period, Helena pointed out that the first period would have no information (unless it had been tied to the last period in history, which Jake's forecast did not do). They turned to Table 3–3 for their review of the line items and information flow.

Line Item	*How the Information Gets There*
Beginning Cash	Calculated: Equals to prior period ending cash
Gross profit (Loss)	Calculated: Sum of current period pre-tax profit or loss plus other expense from the five-year income forecast (Table 3–1). For example, in 1992 the five-year income statement forecasts $305,838 pre-tax profit + $39,600 other expense = $345,438 gross profit.
(Interest Expense)	Calculated: Taken directly from "other expense" on the income statement. It is negative because it represents an outflow of cash.
(Tax Expense)	Calculated: Taken directly from "taxes" on the income statement. It is a negative because it represents an outflow of cash.

(Increase)Decrease to A/R	Calculated: *Negative* sum of current period accounts receivable minus prior period receivables. An *increase* to receivables in the current period compared to the prior period is a *decrease* to cash; therefore the (Increase) to receivables is shown in parentheses to indicated that it is a decrease to cash. Conversely, a decrease in receivables since the last period will increase cash. For example, the 1992 decrease to receivables is ($483,612 − $517,361) × (−1) = $33,749. This decrease is an addition to cash because receivables were collected to effect the decrease.
(Increase)Decrease to Inventory	Calculated: Negative sum of current period inventory minus prior period inventory. A *decrease* to inventory in the current period compared to the prior period is an *increase* to cash since inventory was sold.
(Increase)Decrease to fixed assets	Calculated: Negative sum of current period fixed assets minus prior period fixed assets. An *increase* to fixed assets in the current period compared to the prior period is a *decrease* to cash.
Increase(Decrease) to draw on line of credit	Calculated: Current period draw on credit line minus prior period draw on line. A decrease in the draw on line of credit over the prior period is a decrease to cash. Note that any increase in liabilities and equity is an increase to cash; any increase in assets is a decrease to cash.

Increase(Decrease) to accounts payable	Calculated: Current period accounts payable minus prior period payables. A *decrease* to payables over the prior period is a decrease to cash.
Increase(Decrease) to long-term debt	Calculated: Current period long-term debt minus prior period long-term debt. An increase to long-term debt over the prior period is an increase to cash.
Increase(Decrease) to paid in stock	Calculated: Current period paid in stock minus prior period paid in stock. An increase to paid in stock over the prior period is an increase to cash.
Ending cash	Calculated: Sum of all of the elements from beginning cash through and including increase(decrease) to paid in stock.

Forecasting the Next Five Years at Superdisk

Having produced the forecasting mechanism with Helena, Jake now had to decide how to fill in the variables marked "numerical estimates by Jake."

To start the planning process, Jake called a series of meetings with his marketing and sales staff. The gross sales line in the income statement was forecast after detailed analysis on a product-by-product basis of Superdisk sales potential. Manufacturing agreed to decrease returns as a percentage of gross sales. In prior years information about returns had not been fed back to manufacturing, but for the future Jake and manufacturing management agreed to watch their "performance to plan."

Manufacturing was also given budget responsibility for the cost of goods sold. Like the sales management, manufacturing management made a detailed forecast of product cost. Of course, they had to have the sales forecast complete before they could begin their work, and they had to make assumptions about the purchase of new and replacement equipment, which are a major factor in forecasting fixed assets.

In addition to reviewing their target contributions to income-producing elements of the plan, Jake reviewed spending limits for each of the four operating expense departments and overhead expenses in manufacturing.

Moving to the balance sheet forecast, Jake predicted paid in stock and long-term debt would remain constant during the plan. The long-term debt was money that he and other key founders of the company had lent. The plan accounted for interest on the debt, but there weren't sufficient earnings to repay principal on the long-term financing during the five-year plan. He therefore assumed he would renegotiate the long-term debt. Likewise, Jake preferred not to sell stock until Superdisk once again had a strong history of performance and could sell stock at a decent price.

The fixed asset forecast was a combination of cost estimates for new and replacement equipment for manufacturing necessary to meet sales goals plus a small increment of new and replacement office equipment.

Having made and input all of the predicted data into the forecasts, Jake noted fluctuations in ending cash. Because of the integrated nature of the plan, Jake was able to draw on (and repay) the line of credit to bring cash into a comfortable range for each of the periods.

Using the Cash Flow Forecast to Monitor Performance

Because of the interrelated nature of the plan, reviewing the cash flow forecast is a simple way to identify items to be tracked when monitoring performance. What Jake was looking for were large positive and negative numbers. These would be the "control points" to watch in monitoring performance to his plan.

Gross profit, of course, was the largest number, and the way to monitor that number was to monitor all elements of the income statement forecast. Department production and expense budgets, as well as pricing and related cost of goods sold, were the elements he would have to track.

Interest expense was very important in the early part of the plan, but it became less important later in terms of absolute magnitude.

Tax expense was a large and continuous drain on cash, but only to the extent the profits were realized.

Increasing accounts receivable, incurred as Superdisk grew, were a large and expected user of cash. The growth-induced increases to inventory paralleled receivables growth as a cash user, since receivables are sold inventory.

Fixed assets expanded to provide more capacity to satisfy expanding sales.

Changes to cash induced by changes in the draw on the line of credit reflected the overall volatility of the plan, but they allowed ending cash to remain relatively stable. This perspective will be very important to the banker (or other financial source) trying to understand the cash needs of the company projected by the plan. A more volatile plan is often more risky.

Finally, the contribution to cash made by increasing accounts payable in the last three years of the plan showed how important it was to maintain good supplier credit.

People Make Plans Succeed, Not Numbers

Helena emphasized that the performance of the company depended upon what Jake's people were motivated to do; they would help or impede the success of the plan. Jake had to communicate the plan and set up rules of operation for the plan to be successful. Jake had to learn how to financially control the renewed company. In addition to his persuasive ability, Jake knew that he had to lay out the "rules of the game" in a logical sequence. This process entailed budgeting for objectives and producing an operations manual, both of which are discussed in the next chapter.

CHAPTER 4

Implementing
the
Turnaround

Chapter 3 illustrated in detail how to forecast income, balance sheet information, and cash flow. In this chapter you will learn how to systematically implement the changes and the plans. Until objectives are communicated, measured, enforced, and incentives are produced to encourage managers to participate in the turnaround plan, the turnaround is at risk.

You will follow Jake and Helena as they formulate a budget and budget control technique for the company. The concept of management of objective (MBO) will be introduced as a simple way to tie company planning objectives to departmental objectives and pay rewards to managers. Helena will suggest that three income and expense budgets be made for the company: (1) for sales and returns, (2) for manufacturing, which will control inventory levels and cost of goods sold, and (3) for operating expenses of the company. There will be supplementary budgets for the following balance sheet items: levels of accounts receivable, accounts payable, long-term debt, equity, and fixed assets. All of these items will be tied to the five-year financial forecast, and a manager will be made responsible for each line item in the budget.

The budgets are not the only controlling source for the company. They should be accompanied by an operating manual. Jake will compile a simple operating manual out of existing memos and manuals. In this way Jake can institutionalize the changes that his analysis indicates are necessary to turn Superdisk around.

Management Accountability

For an action-oriented manager like Jake, budgeting was not one of his favorite tasks, but he knew he had to do it to retain control of the turnaround. Nevertheless, he hoped Helena could make the budgeting process as simple and straightforward as possible. Helena assured him it would be straightforward. In fact, one of the principles of budgeting in a small manufacturing company is that the budget should be as simple and limited in scope as possible to get the desired results. Management time is a scarce commodity in a small business, and excessively detailed budgeting and analytical work is not desired.

The company budget, according to Helena, is actually several interrelated budgets: sales, inventory, cost of goods sold, operating expenses, capital requirements, and cash. In management by objectives budgeting, each line in the budgets becomes an objective of an individual manager. (See Tables 4–2 and 4–3 for an example of a sales manager's MBO budget.) Responsibility is given to a manager

TABLE 4–1

Required Company Budgets

- Sales
- Inventory
- Cost of goods sold
- Operating expenses
- Capital requirements
- Cash

for each account in the company's chart of accounts. Resources to attain the objectives are provided and controlled by mutual agreement between the managers and the CEO in a small company. Cash incentives are provided for successful attainment of objectives.

Helena told Jake that financial planning and MBO implementation should feed back on each other. This feedback loop is diagrammed in simple flow chart in Fig. 4–1. Initial objectives for the financial plan must be set up by the CEO. These assumptions are used to produce the financial forecast. The dollar amounts in the forecast become the targets for MBO. But, since MBO requires negotiated agreement between the managers and the CEO, that negotiation process will normally produce changes to the plan that become modifications to the forecast assumptions. This loop is traced as many times as necessary, until all agree on MBO objectives and until the corporate financial plan is acceptable to the CEO.

The Budget Team

Helena suggested that in a small company like Superdisk, it might be wise to form a budget team composed of managers who have the ability to make spending decisions and commit company labor resources.

The budget team at Superdisk was four people: Jake, the CEO; Maura, the marketing manager; Bill, the manufacturing manager; and Joan, the accounting manager. Jake took responsibility for operating expenses and capital requirements. Maura was given the sales budget. Inventory and cost of goods sold belonged to Bill, and Joan had responsibility for monitoring the cash budget and controlling the accounts receivable and accounts payable budgets.

The Marketing Budget

Beginning with gross sales, Jake and Maura sat down and looked at the target of $3,777,564 for 1991 (see Table 3–1). Al-

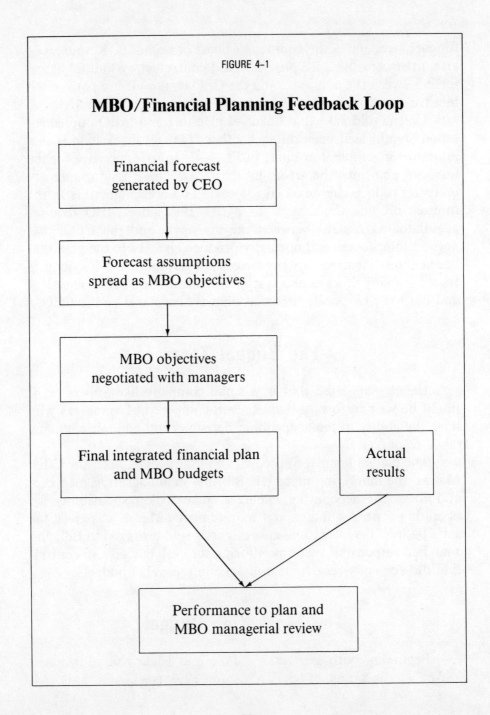

FIGURE 4–1

MBO/Financial Planning Feedback Loop

though it was a smaller amount than 1990 because of the emergency cash control activities, it remained a difficult target because Jake had removed the cables and connector product line and because sales of the full-size disk were projected to drop following a price increase and elimination of the cables and connectors product. Since much of the reduction in full-size disk sales was the result of price increase, Maura will have to work just as hard to produce the smaller volume of sales as she would to produce the full sales volume at a lower price. Jake and Maura worked out a plan that Maura thought she could accomplish with her resources, and Jake provided commission incentives for her to make the targeted amounts (Table 4–2).

Tracking Sales Performance

The detailed sales forecast by product line is an essential part of sales planning but it is not the only part. It is also necessary to track performance to the plan. Jake and Maura worked up a simple sales budget (Table 4–3) that spread the year into monthly sales targets, actual accomplishments to date, and the variation from the goal. Maura's most important objective is to make the cumulative variance come out positive by year's end.

Redefining the Product Mix

One of the problems that had necessitated a turnaround at Superdisk was the drift from a gross margin of 38.9% in 1986 to only 32.1% in 1990 (see Table 2–1). A key to the success of the marketing plan lay in changing the product mix to obtain the 38.06% gross margin that Superdisk required in 1991 to meet its financial objectives, and to establish a foundation for improving gross margin to 44.06% by 1995 (see Table 3–1).

TABLE 4–2

1991 Sales Forecast by Product (in Thousands of Dollars)

	Jan	Feb	Mar	Apr	May	Jun	Jul	Aug	Sep	Oct	Nov	Dec
Full-size disk	110	100	100	100	100	90	90	90	50	40	30	20
Half-size disk	70	100	90	90	120	110	130	150	150	180	190	222.6
Backup tape drive	80	70	70	70	75	70	75	80	70	80	80	80
Supplies	30	30	30	25	30	30	30	30	30	30	30	30
Total Monthly Sales	290	300	290	285	325	300	325	350	300	330	330	352.6
Total 1991 Sales	290	590	880	1,165	1,490	1,790	2,115	2,465	2,765	3,095	3,425	3,777.6

TABLE 4–3

1991 Sales Budget (in Thousands of Dollars)

	Jan	Feb	Mar	Apr	May	Jun	Jul	Aug	Sep	Oct	Nov	Dec
Monthly budget	290	300	290	285	325	300	325	350	300	330	330	352.6
Cumulative budget	290	590	880	1,165	1,490	1,790	2,115	2,465	2,765	3,095	3,425	3,778
Monthly actual	284	312	301	225	311	335						
Cumulative actual	284	596	897	1122	1433	1768						
Monthly variance	−6	12	11	−60	−14	35						
Cumulative variance	−6	6	17	−43	−57	−22						

Assigning Marketing's MBO

All sales for which Maura was responsible were additions to the sales order backlog. An important rule in budgeting for MBO is to divide the work in such a way that the manager responsible for a goal has the resources to achieve it under his or her control. If, for instance, Maura had been made responsible for sales invoiced, her commission and performance would have become dependent upon the success of the manufacturing effort getting product out the door.

Having established a detailed sales forecast by product line (Table 4–2) that fit the first year of the five-year plan, Jake now had to work out an agreement with Maura that would function within the resources budgeted for marketing and sales, and that would serve as an incentive to equal or exceed the sales budget (Table 4–3). Jake decided to reserve 10% of the amount allotted for sales expense for performance incentives.

Maura complained that the one day per month that she would have to spend reviewing the budget could be better spent selling company products, but Jake was firm in his requirement that close monitoring was now the rule.

Management by objectives requires constant and careful monitoring, but the time that such planning and reporting requires will be more than made up in the higher profits typical of a well-managed company. In reality, Maura's perception that the monthly review would take an entire day was unduly pessimistic. As the procedure becomes institutionalized, key performance measurements of the company take very little time to review, and they will give invaluable early warning of problems and opportunities.

Jake knew that as CEO, he had ultimate responsibility to enforce the discipline required to budget and manage by objectives. Without strong leadership on budgeting, Superdisk's financial goals simply wouldn't be achieved.

Controlling Inventory

Bill, the manufacturing manager, was next to visit Jake's office, as Jake worked his way down the income statement, assigning responsibility for cost of goods sold and manufacturing overhead. Bill will also have responsibility for inventory levels on the balance sheet. Like most manufacturing managers, Bill was quite aware of the need for budgeting and welcomed the additional controls on the company financial activity.

Standard Costs

Bill understood that standard valuations for inventories items were set by accounting and that accounting alone could change them with approval of the CEO. A "standard value" or "standard cost" for an inventory item is simply how much that item cost. There are many ways to set such standards which result in varying cost structures for inventory. These cost structures affect profit and tax. Bill often challenged those standards wherever his actual experience showed accounting's valuation to be incorrect.

Each year Superdisk did a physical inventory to obtain an accurate count of raw materials, store materials, work in process, and finished goods. On the basis of this count, production control adjusted its files and keep a running count as the year continued. When a standard cost was applied to an accurate inventory count, a reliable income statement and balance sheet could be produced. There is no way to provide accurate financial management information without accurate inventory valuation.

Jake instructed Joan, the accountant, to prepare a control scheme for the physical inventory. Joan used a checklist suggested by Jerome V. Bennett in his book *Administering the Company Accounting Function* (2nd ed., Englewood Cliffs, N.J.: Prentice-Hall,

1981). Bennett's list included the following points for inclusion in written instructions to the inventory team:

1. Date and time allocated for inventory taking.
2. Name of inventory supervisor.
3. Names and duties of inventory team members.
4. Proper classification of items to be inventories.
5. Physical housekeeping required prior to the inventory.
6. Clear statement of item locations and who has responsibility to count them.
7. Method of identification of items.
8. Description of forms, tag color codes, and marking methods.
9. Instructions on how to use tags and forms.
10. Method to determine quantities that vary with item inventories. For instance, steel washers may be counted by the pound; silver washers may be counted by the piece.
11. Means of verifying count.
12. Details of accounting check (*i.e.,* how to verify that everything that should be counted has been assigned to be counted).
13. Cutoff times and work flow adjustments during inventory.
14. Distribution of serially numbered inventory counting forms.
15. Means for marking an item once counted.

Product Costing

Once the physical inventory is completed, standard costing values are assigned by accounting on the basis of history for each of the items inventories. Any change in the standard valuation of an item had to be accompanied by detailed analysis and approved by accounting.

Accounting did its costing in the following manner. The materials were entered at cost and direct labor was applied at standard rates for each item. Manufacturing overhead, such as manufacturing management salaries, utilities, maintenance, etc., was distributed over the units produced on the basis of labor content in each unit.

Incentives to Minimize Inventory

Jake devised salary incentives for Bill that rewarded Bill for meeting ship dates with a minimum amount of inventory. Manufacturing wanted to have an unlimited inventory for convenience, but a large inventory absorbs working capital and reduces the return on investment (see Figure 4–2). Here's how to use Fig. 4–2: Assume for a moment that accounts receivable, cost of sales, and current liabilities remain constant while additions to inventories are made. Every increase in inventory requires an increase in working capital and, therefore, in total investment. If sales remained constant, then turnover rate is decreased which, in turn, decreases return on investment.

Alternatively, if working capital cannot be increased, an increase in inventory investment will decrease cash and put pressure on collecting receivables from valued customers.

Like Maura, Bill had a target amount in the budget for his departmental expenses. Bill's budget was a great deal more complex than any of the others in the company because of the large number of financial factors that manufacturing had to manage. Budgets were drawn up for total inventory and for each of its components. Budgets were also put in place for manufacturing overhead expenses and for cost of goods sold. As he did with Maura, Jake set up a monthly meeting to discuss each of the budget targets with Bill.

Accounting Budget Responsibilities

Joan, the accountant, was given control of the cash budget as well as target for accounts receivable and accounts payable. Like

FIGURE 4-2

Components of Return on Investment

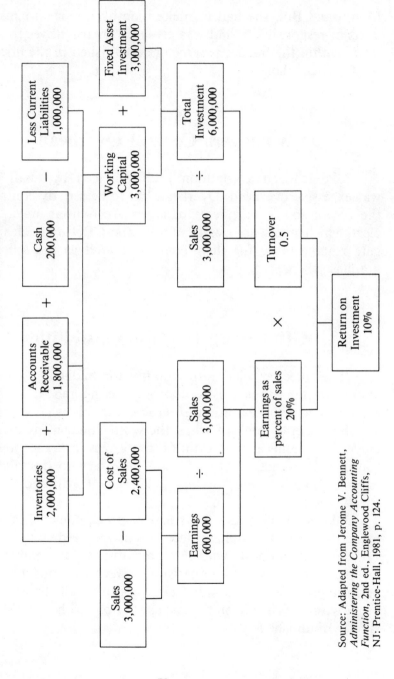

Source: Adapted from Jerome V. Bennett, *Administering the Company Accounting Function*, 2nd ed., Englewood Cliffs, NJ: Prentice-Hall, 1981, p. 124.

Maura and Bill, she had to make monthly reports to Jake in his areas of responsibility and was given salary incentives to keep her items within the budget parameters established in the first year of the five-year plan.

Managers Control Overhead

Jake realized a common problem faced by small business was excessive overhead. Overhead has to be strictly controlled by the responsible department manager. Accounting must make it clear which items are overhead, and the CEO must clearly delegate responsibility for their control as well as the authority to purchase them.

CEO Budgeting Responsibilities

Jake took personal responsibility for budgeting general and administration expense as well as engineering and R&D expenses. General and administration expense control is what most nonaccounting people think of when the word "budget" is used. It includes such items as rent, utilities, employees insurance, telephone, travel, and as many others as are necessary to describe all the "non-production" and "non-capital" ways in which the company spends money.

Jake controlled the fixed assets, or equipment, budget and made the lease or purchase decisions as required.

Jake met monthly with the three other team members so that he could make a direct comparison between the budget and actual performance. Superdisk was under control and directed toward profit within cash capability. The spectre of another meltdown was greatly diminished.

Preparing an Operations Manual

Jake had one final task to complete the turnaround. He had to produce an operations manual for Superdisk.

Operations manuals are an easy reference for all the employees in a company to define rules and procedures. A good operations manual will serve as a tool to help managers and supervisors administer the personnel policies of a company, and it will promote even-handed management throughout the organization, even when individual management style is considerably varied. The operations manual will contain copies of the various forms and documents used in the daily business of the company.

Lines of authority and responsibility are clearly defined in the manual, making it possible for all employees to understand where they fit in the organization. As such, the operations manual becomes a teaching tool for new employees, and a source of internal law and principle for discipline when necessary. When new employees finished reading the operations manual, they would know what was expected of them as an employee of Superdisk, how to communicate with other employees, and who was in charge of what. Ideally, the operations manual would put everything on a businesslike basis at Superdisk.

Jake began to design his operations manual by thinking about items that would normally be included in any operations manual, no matter how large or small the company (see Table 4–4). As he finished his list, Jake realized that many of these policies required frequent updating, so the proper format for the operations manual was a small loose-leaf notebook so he could easily send updates to employees.

In addition to spelling out company policy and procedure, the operations manual served as a tool for communicating long-term company plans and for imbedding them in the company culture. While the operations manual obviously does not have as high a priority as regaining financial control, it must be given enough

TABLE 4–4

Elements of an Operations Manual

1. Statement of purpose for Superdisk.

2. Organization chart.

3. List of employees and job title and to whom they report.

4. Employee relations policy.

5. Pay, health and retirement benefits, leave, and vacation policy.

6. State and federal laws related to workers and workplace.

7. Customer and vendor relation policies, ethics.

8. Discipline and grievance policy.

9. Description of products.

10. Employee responsibilities for quality.

11. Paperwork procedures.

12. Patent, copyright, secrecy, and plant security policy.

13. EPA, OSHA laws related to identifying and disposal of toxics.

14. Safety and medical emergency policy.

15. Maintenance, repair, and employee use of company equipment.

16. Budget policy.

attention to become an effective tool. The issues addressed in the operations manual tend to have long-term or indirect effect on the financial performance of the company.

With his plan in place for Superdisk's turnaround, Jake was ready to consider recapturing the sales that he had been forced to abandon while regaining control of the company and its cash flow. For some time now, Jake had being thinking about how a new product could revitalize Superdisk. Unlike the last new product, which nearly destroyed Superdisk because it was financed with the short-term credit line, Jake was going to plan all aspects of this one.

CHAPTER 5
Finding Informal Sources of Capital for a New Product or Company

With the phasing out of two of Superdisk's product lines—the full-size disk and the cables and connectors—and with the goal of increasing gross margin by 16% by 1995, Jake knew he had to get a new product going soon, and he needed new capital to finance it. Banks or venture capitalists were probably out of the question, because they rarely invested in anything other than established concerns that have proven profit potential. Jake's best option—and the best first option for any new venture—was to raise capital from informal sources.

This and the following two chapters discuss methods of raising capital. Chapter 5 will cover how to obtain informal capitalization. One way is to sell stock beyond the circle of founders, and a sample Offering Memorandum, which is required by law to sell stock in a private offering, is included in the appendix. Raising informal debt capital among friends and associates is also discussed here. Chapter 6 explains how to write the business plan necessary to obtain formal investment from banks or professional financiers, and Chapter 7 describes the formal markets for capital.

In this chapter you will learn some of the practical ways to *informally* sell stock in a new company. Informal sources of capital are found among family, friends, and business associates. As it is used here, "informal" means obtaining capital from sources that are not professionally organized to provide capital. To obtain informal capital you must nevertheless follow a very formal set of rules put forth by the Securities and Exchange Commission and various state agencies. A review of the Offering Memorandum in the Appendix will show how SEC Regulation D, Rule 144 is employed in an unregistered offering.

A registered offering requires expensive financial document preparation and an expensive, full-scale accounting audit of the company. Rule 144 allows companies to raise up to $500,000 without registration. It is most useful to start-up companies because existing companies usually cannot keep their capital requirements below the $500,000 Rule 144 ceiling. Therefore, when existing companies sell stock it is usually to venture capitalists or, less frequently, in public offerings, which are discussed later in this book.

Capitalizing a new firm in the informal markets often involves several stages. The initial stage is most risky and often involves capitalization (sale of stock) in exchange for contributions of time (sweat equity) and equipment, with cash being an extremely scarce commodity. The founders of the company are not required to produce a stock offering memorandum, but it is wise to do so in most cases and their company must file stock sale records with some states when stock is sold. The 83 (b) tax election must be taken within thirty days of the original sale of stock to founders to defer tax liability until the stock is sold, regardless of whether or not an offering is made. The 83 (b) election is discussed below.

After the initial organization has taken place, a stock offering memorandum must be produced for your private investors, and the investors must pay cash. Start-up companies often rely on private individual investors at first because of the speed with which they are able to invest. Only much later, after the company has developed the product to the point of profitability, do formal sources of capital come into play. (An exception to this rule may be certain high-powered companies seeking very rapid growth. They might go directly to a venture capitalist for funds.)

Early in the company's formation, a decision should be made as to whether there is enough interest among the group of private investors to support the product to the point of self-sustaining profitability. The reason for this is that professional venture capital is hesitant to invest in a company with a large group of private stockholders, unless it has attained self-sustaining profitability. (The venture capitalists' hesitancy stems from a fear of liability to the private stockholder group if profitability is not reached. It is also more difficult to sway the opinion of a larger group of private stockholder on board decisions.)

Jake's New Company Idea

For a number of years Jake had been considering diversifying his company into the area of tele-presence for education and entertainment. Tele-presence equipment allows a viewer in a distant place to see in perfect three-dimensions what a remote camera was recording. Rather than trying to stay on the forefront of research and development, which is what manufacturing of tele-presence equipment would require, Jake decided that he would rather purchase state-of-the-art equipment and build his business around applications software and programming for this new equipment.

Stone Soup

Once again, Jake decided to ask Helena, his financial analyst friend, for her perspective on starting a new company. Helena said that attracting new investors was like selling stone soup, and to explain she related this Russian folk tale:

Three hungry peasants were traveling through a village in which everyone was so poor that no one could spare them a scrap of food for supper. In fact, each barely had enough to feed himself.

Not despairing, one of the travelers suggested to his companions that they make "stone soup." He pulled a kettle from his pack, filled it with water, built a fire under it, and put in three nice stones from a nearby brook. The villagers had by then gathered around his fire, wondering what he was cooking. "Stone soup," he replied. "It's really delicious, but I don't have enough here to share." One villager volunteered her three carrots for a share, another a few potatoes, yet another a bone with some meat on it. And so, everyone seeking a share put what he had into the pot, and soon the whole village sat down to the best soup they had eaten in months.

Helena said that Jake's job would be not unlike that of the hungry travelers: he would have to create as much value in his start-up venture as he could without actual cash investments. This would be done through the "sweat equity" of the founding investors and through exchanging stock for equipment. Other investors can then be attracted when it can be demonstrated to them that the founders have already made significant and effective investments in the venture.

Creating Value

Helena and Jake sat down together to review how to recruit founding investors and create value in the new operation. A summary of Helena's advice follows:

One of the central objectives of starting your company must be to have it sufficiently capitalized. Capital comes from two sources—your own pockets or the pockets of investors.

Another objective of starting the company is to have control of the company remain with the founders until they are ready to trade that control for money. Of course, once this happens, the founders are working for the stockholders, and they have relinquished their freedom to direct the company for monetary rewards.

In order to attract other people's money after the initial funding stage of the company, one of the things that all potential investors look for is how much the founders have invested. Are the founders willing to put their money where their mouths are? There are several techniques often employed to "create value" in start-up companies. These methods are perfectly ethical and legal, and yet they offer the founders the ability to "invest" in their company with very little cash and very little risk.

Exchanging Equipment for Stock

In the formation stage of the company, founders can purchase stock by trading tangible items for the stock, such as machinery, office furniture, etc. These items legally belong to the corporation and show as assets on its books. If they are put into the company at fair market value, these items cannot be questioned later as the source of paying for our founders stock. A simple bill of sale in exchange for stock is all that is required.

Sweat Equity Becomes Stock

There is also a way to capitalize the valuable contribution of time. The method is simply this: the principals in the new company set a reasonable rate for their hours as consultants to the company. They then submit a monthly billing to the company clearly defining what they have done that will create or enhance the value of a tangible asset of the company. For example, a hypothetical co-founder might incur organization costs such as incorporating the company. Another hypothetical co-founder might create lines of programming and complete modules for a software product. Co-founders may allow these billings to accumulate until they are worth, for example, $10,000. They then purchase a unit of the stock offering by writing the company a $10,000 check to pay for their consulting time. The resulting accounting transaction is a wash, effectively converting consulting hours into stock ownership. To the benefit of the new company, the company is able to purchase valuable work for shares of stock without using cash, and it creates an expense to decrease income tax liability for the firm when sales occur.

What have the founders accomplished with these transactions?

First, they have created a tax liability for themselves, which means that if things don't go according to plan they will have to pay Uncle Sam whatever percentage of the $10,000 income that they owe him. If, by December 31, the startup is not a going concern, they close the company. This causes them to lose their "investment" in stock, and they have a tax write-off that exactly matches their tax liability for consulting income. Assume, however, that the company has developed a product and is able to gain significant amounts of new financing through sale of an offering. Assume further that the founders have created an asset on their personal net worth statement of $285,000 with an initial investment of $15,000 ($10,000 consulting plus $5,000 contributed equipment), and that in the subsequent offering shares sold for $1.00 per share. (The Appendix contains a sample Offering Memorandum, required for new stock issues by the Securities and Exchange Commission and by various state securities departments.)

As an example, assume that there are four founding investors: John, Flint, Rita, and Terry, and that each contributes furniture and equipment worth $5,000. This amounts to a total of 400,000 shares for tangible assets traded for stock initially valued at $0.05 per share. Assume also that John and Flint work fulltime in the company, each trading $10,000 worth of labor for an additional 400,000 shares total. Each founder has now made the following investment:

Founder	Contribution	Founder's Shares
John	$15,000	300,000
Flint	$15,000	300,000
Rita	$ 5,000	100,000
Terry	$ 5,000	100,000

If the offering can be sold some months later at $1.00 per share, John and Flint would each reap a $285,000 paper profit ($300,000 less $15,000 investment). *None of their investment was cash.*

This value creation for the founders is predicated upon the secondary investors in the offering being convinced that shares in the company are worth $1.00 per share. The process is identical to the process of blue-chip stock appreciation of the largest companies. In the case of a start-up company, increase in value comes from having organized, capitalized, and begun product development in the company. It is also created by the second-stage investors when they make their investment in the company at the asking price of the stock.

The dilution (paying $1.00 per share when founders paid only $0.05) is explained as a risk in the offering memorandum (see the section on risk factors in the sample offering memorandum in the appendix), and it generally will not discourage a sophisticated investors who believes the financial forecast for the company. So long as the investor's return on investment is projected to be sufficient (26% per year compounded is average), the investor will accept the dilution as a means of providing strong, sheltered, long-term, financial incentives for the founding principals. And, after all, it will be the long hours, hard work, and dedication of its founders that will convert the company and its stock into a valuable asset and establish the company's credibility for potential investors.

Jake's head was spinning with the possibilities of creating wealth with no cash investment. Helena brought him back to reality with the reminder that all that had been accomplished so far was to put the stones in the pot (that is, Jake was the sole founder yet subscribing). To complete the recipe for stone soup, an offering of stock at $1.00 per share for cash had to succeed. This sale of stock would provide the money to convert his idea for Newcorp into a going concern.

83 (b) Election Defers Capital Gains Liability

Helena also told Jake about the 83 (b) election (Fig. 5–1), which should be considered by the founders. By submitting an 83 (b) election to the IRS (and to some states where required) within 30 days of the original sale of stock to founders, a founder may defer taxation on capital gain until the stock is actually sold.

Otherwise, and this is not widely known, a founder's tax lia-

FIGURE 5–1

Election to Include Property Transferred in Connection with Services Performed in Gross Income Pursuant to Section 83 (B) Internal Revenue Code

Instructions to Persons Filing This Form:

1. File one copy of this form with the Internal Revenue Service Center where you file your tax return within thirty days of the transfer of property to you.

2. Include one copy of this form with your tax return for the taxable year in which the property was transferred.

3. Submit one copy to the person for whom you have performed any services for which you received the property.

4. Retain one copy for your records.

Section 83 (b) Election:

1. Your name: _____

   Your address: _____

   Your Taxpayer Identification No.: _____
   (Individuals should fill in their Social Security Number.)

2. A description of each property with respect to which this election is being made: _____

3. The date or dates on which the property covered by this election were transferred to you: _____

   Taxable year of election: _____
   (Individuals should fill in calendar year in which property was transferred to them.)

4. Describe the nature of the restrictions on transfer, such as vesting schedules, to which the property is subject: _____

5. State the fair market value, at the time of its transfer to you, of each property for which this election is made: _____

6. Describe the amount, if any, paid for such property: _____

7. I certify that a copy of this statement has been furnished to any person or persons for whom I have performed services with respect to such property and to any person who transferred such property to me if not the same as the person for whom I have performed services. The persons to whom I have provided copies are as follows:

   _____

   I state that I have made the foregoing election pursuant to Section 83 (b) of the Internal Revenue Code.

   _____
   Signature of Person
   Making Election

   _____
   Print Name of Person
   Making Election

bility for the difference between the acquisition price, $0.05, and its next valuation, $1.00, creates a tax liability for which the company is obligated to issue a 1099 form to the founder. (Such a valuation might occur upon subsequent issue of stock if there was no initial gain.) The increased valuation represents a taxable capital gain.

If a firm neglects to issue a 1099 for this transaction, as often occurs out of ignorance, it can haunt a company wanting to go public. Such an omission will not pass a Big 8 accounting firm audit, and, at that point, the founders are not only liable for the tax, but for penalties for late payment.

Jake's Informal Stock Offering

After he returned to his office at Superdisk, Jake began to put together a list of friends, relatives, and business associates who might be interested in a Newcorp offering. The list was not as long as he imagined it would be. There were reasons not to include many of his friends and relatives who were not able to withstand the loss of their investment if Newcorp failed. As a matter of personal preference, Jake decided to exclude all of his family and friends except those he knew were active investors in seed capital companies. This exclusion significantly shortened his list.

But as he thought about it, the list really extended a great deal further than it appeared on the surface. Of the three dozen people he had chosen to contact, about a third of them were lawyers, bankers, or other small businessmen, each with his or her own network of friends and business associates. If they became interested enough to purchase the stock, they could introduce him to other qualified investors to whom he could make the offering.

(In 1988, a report funded by the Small Business Association [*The Informal Supply of Capital* by Robert J. Gaston and Sharon E. Bell] showed that individual private investors put an estimated $64.2 billion into small businesses around the United States compared to the $4 billion invested in small companies by professional venture capital. Gaston and Bell found that the individual investors were typically looking for a 26% return on their investment each year, but that they were willing to leave it in the company in the form of equity for five to seven years. That study and a recently published book by Dr. Gaston, *Finding Private Venture Capital for Your Firm: a Complete Guide* [New York: Wiley, 1989], are unique profilings of informal sources of capital for the reader interested in obtaining this type of funding.)

It was crucial for Jake to talk to legal counsel before selling Newcorp stock in order to gain a clear understanding of to whom he could make an offer.

Networking is the way in which potential offerees are found, and friends of friends can be a very powerful way to greatly extend a network. Note, however, that the Securities and Exchange Commission (SEC) has detailed rules and regulations intended to keep a company from making an unregistered "public" offering by broadcast advertising to the general public.

After a complete review of his potential investors list, Jake figured that he could raise several hundred thousand dollars of informal capital from his family and business associates. Helena recommended that Jake consult a lawyer specializing in business law to draw up an offering memorandum (see appendix). Even though obtaining capital from friends and associates is called "informal" (meaning direct or without formal intermediaries), the SEC and the various state control the sale of corporate stock very closely. Each state has a different set of rules and regulations regarding the sale and offering of stock, and the SEC rules are modified both by case law and tax law with great frequency. An offering memorandum, therefore, is *not* a do-it-yourself project for most small business owners.

The lawyer Jake chose spent several hours explaining how to qualify investors and how to take subscriptions. In addition, the lawyer agreed to serve as escrow agent for the funds until the minimum amount had been subscribed and to handle all required reporting of the sale of stock transactions with the state and the SEC.

Regulation D

Jake's lawyer explained some of the reasons for utilizing Regulation D as a guide for making the offering. Regulation D, Rule 144 refers to the SEC rules and regulations allowing relatively simple, unregistered stock offerings of up to $500,000 to up to 35 financially qualified and experienced investors. As a means of avoiding some of stringent reporting requirements for registered public offerings, equity offerings to 35 or fewer sophisticated investors can be viewed as private placements and therefore subject only to state laws regulating the private sale of stock.

Purchasers of private offerings must be accredited investors, meaning they must meet certain net worth, income requirements, and investment experience requirements. This protects the smaller investor from getting involved in private placement transactions that he cannot afford or that he does not have the expertise to evaluate. (An "offeree questionnaire" appears in the offering memorandum for Newcorp in the Appendix.)

Because of the high cost of making registered offerings, Regulation D issuers often will try to confine the size of the private offering to $500,000 or less, as specified by Rule 144. For such offerings, legal bills generally run about $10,000 to $15,000 for production of the offering memorandum and filing of the necessary state and federal notifications.

Jake's lawyer warned him that private placements are sometimes difficult to do. This is partly due to the SEC rule that investors in private placements must hold "letter stock" at least two years before liquidating. Letter stock is stock which has resale restrictions printed or typed on the certificate. Because of illiquidity, a successful private placement, therefore, often involves a firm with a product idea that has extraordinary prospects.

Jake decided that Newcorp's product was revolutionary enough to obtain informal capital, and he had a clear idea to whom he would sell each of the units. So he decided to proceed with the offering.

When Informal Equity Isn't Enough

Jake spent almost six months from the time that he started the project to the time that the private investment funds were ready to be used. Helena assured him that he had done a relatively quick offering. While it was a great deal of work to prepare, the offering was not difficult to sell because Jake knew in advance to whom he would offer it.

Jake had $190,000 net in the bank after the offering. With these proceeds Jake was ready to start his new company, but his business plan (described in the next chapter) showed that he would need far more than $190,000 over the first two years in business to capitalize the business adequately. In fact, his successful informal offering had raised only 20% of what he needed.

Since he had exhausted his contacts for raising informal equity, Jake decided to try informal sources of debt. Like his search for equity, Jake had to support his request for a loan with a business plan. Unlike the equity offering, however, this plan had to include several reasonable ways in which the debt could be serviced and repaid. Jake found it a simple matter to put together a one-page fact sheet on his new company's use for the funds, the debt-to-equity-ratios, the requested term and interest rate of the loan, and the means of repayment of the funds.

Unlike the equity offering, the debt offering required much less formal documentation, and Jake was able to offer it to his friends and associates a few days after he conceptualized the deal he would offer. While his friends supported his effort, they had used most of their available funds to purchase the stock offering, and Jake found that his investor group was not a bottomless well of capital. They indicated a willingness to follow their stock investment with a loan, but most of them required a year or more before they could make the loan.

Jake therefore realized that he would have to turn to formal sources of capital to find the remainder of the money necessary to make Newcorp a success. The strategy would be to build upon the capital that he had successfully raised with the private offering.

In the next chapter, Jake will prepare a business plan used to market his firm to professional investors. Then in Chapter 7, Jake will review formal sources of capital. These formal sources will include both debt and professional venture capital sources. He will also learn the difference between "cash-flow-based lenders" and "asset-based lenders." Finally, Jake will examine the narrow range where a Small Business Administration (SBA) loan becomes possible and desirable.

CHAPTER 6

Writing
a Convincing
Business Plan
for Formal
Investors

By now (six months after the private funding) the tele-presence software created by Newcorp shows promise and much of the risk involved in its development is gone. Jake must, therefore, begin the process of obtaining more capital for the growing firm from formal investors. Formal investors require far more detailed information about the company than do the original founders because they do not have first-hand knowledge of the company and because they often must present and defend their investment recommendations to committees.

Chapter 6 will help you develop an effective business plan. A business plan is the preferred, and usually required, format for presenting a company or its new products as an investment opportunity. Obtaining professional venture capital is an extremely competitive activity, and a company's business plan is how it initially distinguishes itself from the competition.

The business plan is generally the only document required to approach professional venture capitalists, although they will want to see much of the material that would be included in an offering memorandum (see appendix) if they become seriously interested in making an investment. Often, an existing company that is adding a product line will seek professional venture capital to develop its new line.

Strategic Planning

Jake of course realized that his proposed new product line, computer software for tele-presence entertainment, was quite a bit different than manufacturing computer hardware. His first strategic decision six months ago was to produce a new company separate from Superdisk.

Before writing a business plan, Jake will consider how to further reduce risks and he will determine what type of return and payback period would be required to attract formal investment. Most important; he will work to obtain software application specifications from his potential customers.

Reducing Start-up Risks

Jake knew in planning a new business or product that the planning process should focus on the lowest-cost path to the point of profit breakeven. Along the way, there will be benchmarks or "watershed developments," after which point the risk of getting to breakeven will be substantially reduced. It was necessary to identify such benchmarks in the plan, because those "risk-reduction points" will form natural funding goals for the company. For example, a company that planned to make an automotive supercharger would have its risk greatly reduced as soon as a prototype was successfully run on the test stand.

Payback and Return on Investment Requirements

Professional venture capitalists vary widely in their payback period requirements, with the older, more stable venture companies willing to make longer investments and some of the newer companies needing to turn around their investments more frequently.

The return sought by professional venture capitalists ranges upward from the 26% compounded annual rate sought by informal investors. Unlike private investors, the professional venture capitalists require larger deals (and often control of the company) before they invest. The professional venture capitalists, in the best case, bring a level of talent to the new company that exceeds the talent and experience of most private investors.

Planning Driven by Customer Needs

Jake's experience had taught him to allow his customers to specify what they will buy and how much they will pay for it. A common mistake among many start-up businesses is to find a source for market information showing the overall size of the market and then to project obtaining a piece of it based upon an internally generated concept of the market. Only the customer can tell the entrepreneur what he wants and needs. Listening to and understanding customer desires is the foundation of small business success.

Jake developed the following checklist to help him structure his market research for a tele-presence product (the offering memorandum in appendix describes his product):

Marketing Research Checklist for Newcorp

1. Who are the customers? Are they end users or others?
2. Where are the customers located?
3. How is a random group selected to test a product idea?
4. How are potential customers approached for information?
5. How is the idea of tele-presence introduced to test it?

6. How are customers asked about applications for tele-presence?

7. How much will customers pay per minute for tele-presence?

8. At what price does a customer prefer tele-presence to movies?

9. Why will a customer use tele-presence programming rather than movies?

10. At what point is professional programming required?

11. What need does tele-presence fill for customers?

12. What can competitors tell me about customers?

13. Are there any trade shows or associations of customers?

14. Where would customers normally read about the products?

15. How will customers use tele-presence?

16. Where will customers use the product?

17. What other competition exists or is likely to arise?

18. What are the cost trade-offs for customer-desired features?

19. Is there any way to test market the idea without hardware?

20. What are the most cost-effective ways to gauge customer wants?

21. Are there demographic influences on the customer base?

22. Are there geographic influences on the customer base?

How to Write a Winning Business Plan

After reviewing his marketing checklist, Jake was ready to produce a formal business plan. He had done several rounds of strategic thinking to convince himself that he had a viable business idea. The business plan bore the more formidable task of convincing investors, who had no direct experience with the company, that the business was worth their risk in financially supporting it.

Once again, Jake called in Helena to help him with the crucial process of presenting his company in a way that would make it attractive to investors.

There are many models available for doing a business plan, but the one that Helena adopted and modified is an outline produced by a major accounting firm. She presented, in annotated outline form, the basic items that Jake had to include for his business plan to be seriously considered. Helena found that this outline had gotten her clients rave reviews (usually a sign that you have a chance for funding) from the professional venture capitalists.

Helena emphasized that the business plan, unlike the company financials, must be prepared by Jake himself. Jake could get help in presenting his plan professionally, but it had to be his own plan or it just wouldn't fly. Before any money would be forthcoming from professional sources, Jake would be thoroughly grilled by them, and Jake would have to know his business plan by heart.

Helena advised Jake to keep his business plan brief and to the point, but to cover all the points in the guidelines, presented on the following pages. (Business plans are usually between 20 and 100 pages, depending on the type of business.)

Part 1: Executive Summary

1. Keep the Summary Short.

Write the executive summary of the business plan last, after finishing all the other parts of the plan. The summary must be brief—two pages at the maximum. The summary will introduce the plan to the venture capitalist who is being asked to capitalize a company. A venture capitalist may literally read through 200 proposals before selecting 10 to investigate further and one or two to actually fund. Writers of business plans should put themselves in the place of the venture capitalist. Who would want to read 200 20-page summaries (4,000 pages), if the same information could be gleaned from 200 2-page summaries (400 pages)?

2. How is the Company Planning to Make Money?

The summary must accurately, but briefly, tell the venture capitalist how he can make abundant profit by investing in your company. Therefore, the first thing a summary must do is convince its reader that the marketplace wants the company's product. After all, isn't that why anyone goes into business, to meet a market need and make a profit doing it?

3. Think of Potential Investors as if They Were Partners.

Write the summary as if the investor is to be a partner in the business. He or she may not be a partner in the legal sense of the word, but the venture capitalist should be viewed as someone who is sharing the profit in return for providing capital.

4. Tell What is Distinctive About the Company and Product.

The summary must set the company's product apart from the competition: why is the marketplace going to buy what your company will sell rather than what its competitor has to sell? If the company is developing a new product, the summary must explain the various stages of the development.

5. Indicate the Important Milestones.

The venture capitalist will be interested in where the development risk goes down in the plan. This does not mean that he won't fund a plan before the risk is gone; it means that he must understand where risk is reduced in determining how much to offer for a piece of the company. The summary should also indicate when the new company or new product is scheduled to reach profitability, and how soon after that the investment will be recovered.

Always keep the summary brief, a maximum of two pages, and focused on how the company is going to make money.

Part 2: Table of Contents

The table of contents follows the form of the business plan outline. It must be clear and direct your reader to the information he or she wants. Imagine that the summary says that XYZ's anti-gravity machine can significantly reduce the rolling friction in freight trains, and that the railroads will purchase them for every freight car in the world. Your reviewer will have questions. What is the company's patent position? Which company is threatened to be put out of business (competitors) if it succeeds? He expects the table of contents to direct him right to the spot in the business plan that will provide him with the detailed information he wants, and the table of contents must serve that purpose.

The table of contents must be well thought out, not just something that is added before rushing to the copy machine to meet the afternoon courier service deadline. Business plan writers must remember that the venture capitalist is under as much time pressure as they are.

Part 3: Description of the Company

The purpose of this short section is to answer the following questions: What is the company's business? What does the company produce or what services does it provide? What are its markets? How are its products and services used?

If these categories sound a lot like major topics to be addressed in the body of the business plan, it's because they are. This section restates in more detail some of the points already made in the summary, but not in so much detail that nothing is left to be revealed in the body of the business plan.

This section must also address what the company does better than anyone else. What is unique about the business that makes it so much better than its competitors? What is it that the company provides better, faster, cheaper, or more valuably to its customers than its competitors can?

This part of the business plan must be written to convince the venture capitalist that the company has something that he will want to share in. *The business plan must convince the venture capitalist that the company has or does something unique and better than anyone else in its field.*

Part 4: Marketing and Sales

The sections on marketing and sales are the heart of the business plan. The financial plan, which integrates all the other aspects of the business plan, is the head. But, without a heart, all the financial wizardry in the world is useless. Marketing and sales determine company income. The company never has a dime more than sales produces. Therefore, funding sources look very closely at the logic and feasibility of the marketing and sales portion of the business plan.

1. Overcoming Marketing's Anti-Planning Bias.

Marketing and sales staff often resist the actually writing of their part of the plan. That's because most great marketing people are sales people, and all great sales people chafe at having to do "paper shuffling and bean counting" rather than spending time with the customer who is the source of orders. An interview technique is often the most effective way to draw out a marketing plan or sales forecast. That is, you develop and ask the questions and write down the marketing person's responses. There are always some blank spots. Good managers see these blank spots as areas needing support and they provide that support: ideas, assignments, the time and travel resources for marketing personnel to get the specific answers needed. The business plan writer should expect to help marketing and sales complete their central part of the business plan, perhaps by doing some research himself.

2. Focus on the Customer's Needs.

Basing product design and all aspects of business upon customer requirements and desires has been used very successfully by the Japanese in worldwide competition. What does the customer want? If the business plan can answer that question convincingly, it will show that the marketing homework has been done. If it cannot, all the supporting research in the world isn't going to help.

3. Characterize the Industry.

The business plan should address the following marketing questions: What industry is the company in? How big is it? How big will it become? Characterize the industry. What are its unique characteristics? Who are the major customers in the company's industry? Predict trends. How will the product be used? How is the market segmented?

4. Market Segmentation.

The market segmentation section addresses the differences and similarities among customers in the market. It is often confused with market share, which is concerned with how the market is divided among the suppliers competing in that market. A market segment might be unmarried males, 18 to 26 years of age, who own automobiles. The plan should show why the company's product is desired by this segment and exactly how this segment can be reached. Ignorance of market segmentation leads to failure of a marketing plan.

5. Regulation and Usage Impact.

Is the market regulated? How? What impact on the plan? What is the economic impact of the product on its purchasers? What changes will the customer have to make to use the product? Is the use of the product going to change in the future?

6. Competition.

Who is the competition? What product lines and services compete with others? How do your customers compare the company's products with competitors products? What is the estimated market share of competitors? Will it change? Will the competitors think they have to destroy the company in order to survive?

7. Marketing Strategy.

What is the marketing strategy? How is the company going to advertise and promote its product? Through what channels will the product be distributed? How are you going to price the product? What product field support is required and how is it to be provided? What are the geographic considerations involved in the plan? How is the company going to sell? How is it going to identify customers?

8. Selling to People Not to Corporations or Companies.

When a sale is made, accounts receivable aging shows the name of the company. Your company will be paid with a check bearing the name of that company. It is easy to make the mistake that the company is the customer. The sale is made when a *person* with buying authority orders the product. That person is the customer, not the company with which he or she is affiliated. Marketing sales plans are most convincing when they describe how the company is going to identify that person who is going to make the decision to buy the product. Therefore, the plan must answer these questions: How is sales going to contact them? How many sales people will this require? What is the sales efficiency per salesman likely to be, and why? What will the order size be? Will there be follow-on orders? How much sales effort will be required for follow on? Quotas? What is the commission plan for the sales people?

The answers to these questions should be quantified in dollars or employee-days of effort, and then checked to see that they make sense financially.

9. Beware of Prejudging a Product's Success.

Being overly optimistic about your product's success can backfire. People tend to try to support what they already believe, rather than looking at what their research is telling them. It is easy for a small business owner enamored with his dream product to overlook what the facts are telling him.

10. The Numbers Trap, or Circular Market Planning.

Another helpful hint in the marketing and sales section of the business plan is to avoid the numbers trap. In other words, the numbers in your marketing and sales plan, no matter how good they sound on paper, are worthless if they haven't been tested against reality, reality being actual market conditions and customers behavior. Listening to the music of one's own voice must be avoided in the business plan.

The numbers trap works something like this. The market for internal combustion engines is $100 billion dollars per year. External combustion "Stirling" engines are one-and-one-half times as efficient as internal combustion engines. ABC Engine Company projects that if the cost of gasoline is $3.00 per gallon, the extra efficiency of its Stirling engine would repay its extra cost of manufacture. In 1980, authorities in energy exploration project gasoline costs of $5.00 per gallon by 1990, increasing at a dollar a year thereafter. (Such assumptions were considered conservative in 1980.) Given the mechanical breakthrough of ABC's Stirling engine it is going to be difficult to hold back the demand for the product to 1% of the market, or a billion dollars per year.

Did ABC Engine Company go ask Ford or GM what they thought about the idea? No. Did they get even one customer to tell them what this engine ought to be like before they spend $100,000 making a prototype? No. Did the price of gasoline go onward and upward past $3.00 per gallon? No. By November, 1988, unleaded gasoline could be purchased at a station above San Francisco for 83.9 cents per gallon. Was ABC's Stirling engine a successful product? No. Did it ever have a *chance* to be successful? No. Over $100,000 were wasted by ABC Engine Company learning this lesson.

Marketing and New product people must learn to go to their customers to get them to specify what it is that they will buy, and *why*.

Part 5: Research and Development

The Market place is rapidly changing. A four-function calculator that cost $300 (adjusted for inflation) in 1973 can be found for $3 today with a square root key and photocell power thrown in for free. A company may have a great product, but the world keeps changing. The purpose of this section of the business plan is to convince a potential investor that the company has what it takes to stay one stride ahead of the pack, particularly if the company is involved in producing a high-technology product.

Answering the following questions will test the understanding of research and development issues facing the company:

How far along is your *next* product (or first product if the company is a start-up). Is there a prototype? Has the company entered production? Does the company have a patent? Has it applied for a patent? What company has better technology? What is the forecast for technological change? Will the company's technology be outdated by the time it hits the market? What are the major projected R&D benchmarks? How is the company going to get to the next generation?

Part 6: Manufacturing

Addressing the following issues related to manufacturing shows how well a company can meet the product demand substantiated in the marketing and sales portion of the plan.

How will the company produce the product? Which parts will be made internally, which parts subcontracted? Does the company have a production advantage? How much capacity does it have? What is needed to expand it? Are there any sole-source suppliers? Are there any parts with long lead times? What are manufacturing overhead absorption rates, and how will they be affected by changes in volume?

Part 7: Ownership and Management

Many venture capitalists claim that they invest in people, not products or plans. People, rather than machines, are seen as the capital of modern information-based companies.

1. People as Capital.
The venture capitalist must be convinced that company managers have enough invested in the company to stay through stressful times, that they have a track record of success, or that the managers have failed and bounced back constructively. If the key management team does not have a green money stake in the business, it is

going to be very difficult to sell any business plan to a venture capitalist or any other sophisticated investor.

The following questions must be answered in a good business plan: Who are the key managers at each position on the company team? What is their ownership incentive on the upside? What has each manager accomplished in the past that relates specifically to making the business profitable? When are you going to fill out the remainder of your team? Can it be proven that company managers are unencumbered legally or ethically with prior employers? Name the board of Directors and tell how each member can contribute to wise, farsighted direction of the company.

2. Identify all "Sophisticated" Investors Clearly.

List current stockholders and those holding conversion rights to the stock. If dozens of stockholders were brought into the corporation through private offerings, the business plan should indicate which of these investors is "sophisticated" as defined by the SEC; anyone with a net worth exclusive of home and furnishings in excess of $1,000,000 is currently considered sophisticated. Check with an attorney specializing in corporate law to get the current definition of other sophisticated investors with net worth less than $1,000,000 (investment experience can be substituted for wealth to some extent).

3. Venture Capitalists Are Wary of Nonprofessional Investors.

As a generalization, venture capitalists like to work with other venture capitalists rather than with a large number of unsophisticated stockholders. Why? Because private individuals tend to be nervous, vocal, unhappy about dilution (owning less of the company as more shares are sold), and more likely to sue. Does this mean that nonprofessional investors and professional venture capital investors are mutually exclusive? No, but it does mean that the relationship has to be finessed.

Advisory boards can improve how investors look. Nonprofessional investors may be made to look better to the venture capitalist if they are making a contribution on the board of directors or on

111

a board of technology advisors to the company. Nonprofessional investors are always more acceptable if they have made a very large investment so they have a lot to lose by putting the company at risk with their actions.

4. What is the Stock Currently Authorized and Issued?

This question has to do with how far ownership can be diluted with future offerings. An aggressive venture capitalist can demand special classes of stock, especially after gaining control of a voting majority of the stock, which can dilute early investors. The only defense to this is that if the venture capitalists go too far in this direction they will find they have to support the company on their own. Fig. 6–1 shows how to present the ownership of the company.

5. Every Investor Should Have a Business Purpose in the Company.

In Fig. 6–1, note how everyone has a place in the list of owners. Everyone is *somebody*. The eleven early nonprofessional investors have become "founders" of the company. Lisa Morgen, who holds no office in the company, is an expert in the technology of lizard skin wallets, the main product of XYZ. She has become a "technical advisor" to the company.

This may seem like a fabrication. It is not. It is putting the company's best foot forward. The company financial managers must make certain that all company investors have a role in the company if possible and provide substantiation with written records.

Note that all the small investors are lumped in a group of founders rather than providing a long and daunting list of minority stockholders. The company will, of course, have on file a stockholder qualification form signed by the investor and the company president, with review noted by the corporate counsel.

Below is shown a hypothetical resume for one of the managers. The resumes of all key managers must be provided, usually as an exhibit in the appendix of the business plan.

FIGURE 6-1

Principal Stockholders and Directors of XYZ Corporation

Stockholder	Shares	Percent
Dr. Bradley Took, Chairman	100,000	6.33
John Gordon III, Director	900,000	56.96
Lisa Morgen, Technical Advisor	150,000	9.49
Brenda Starr, Marketing V.P.	50,000	3.17
Borden Rock, President and Director	200,000	12.66
Torkel Stubbs, Director	25,000	1.58
Joe Smith, Controller	50,000	3.17
Harden Wenks, Founder	25,000	1.58
Ten Founders	80,000	5.06
Total Shares Outstanding	1,580,000	100.00

*Each of these key employees has the right to purchase an equal additional amount of shares for $1.25 per share after remaining in the employ of XYZ Corporation for three years. This option was granted as a condition of employment.

Brenda Starr, Marketing Vice President

Miss Starr has 15 years of experience in marketing, engineering, and sales before she joined XYZ Corporation in April of 1986. She is considered one of the leaders in developing the market for wallets made of exotic animal skins. Miss Starr has been instrumental in developing the new lizard skin wallet line for XYZ, and she currently has responsibility for marketing it. The lizard skin wallet line provides 15% of XYZ sales and 20% of its gross profit margin. The lizard skin wallet line is expected to grow to 50% of the company sales in the next 5 years.

Note that the business plan resume is quite brief and that it highlights the profit contributions made to the company. As mentioned before, brevity without losing content is the key to keeping a venture capitalist interested.

Part 8: The Financial Plan

The financial plan within a business plan is broken into two parts: the verbal description of funds required and use of funds, and the numbers that describe a planned financial future for the company.

The investor will want to have the following questions answered to his satisfaction before considering actual funding:

How much money does the company currently require? How much more money will it require over the next five years, and when will it be needed? How will these funds be deployed? After the company has reached breakeven, how much of these funds can be raised with debt rather than additional equity? Explain what is being offered. How many shares of the company are for sale? What dilution occurs at the price asked?

Don't give a valuation analysis here, but be prepared to support a valuation of the company if a venture capitalist is interested. Be fair, and be firm in your pricing. (Chapter 8 shows how to place a value on the company.) Do the necessary homework before stating an asking price, and be certain that approval of the price by the board of directors is in place before sending out the business plan with an offering price buried in the funds required section.

Finally, tell the potential investor how he is going to be able to cash in at the end of his investment. Is the company going to go public? Is company management going to try to sell the business to another? How is the venture investor going to get his profit out? (Chapter 9 deals with public offerings.)

Part 9: Financial Data

The purpose of the financial data section is to provide the potential investor with the numerical data needed for his analysis of whether or not your company is a good investment.

Financial data falls into two categories, historical and forecast. The plan should include at least three years of your annual historical financials (see Chapter 2). Also bind into the business plan a copy of the most recent monthly financials. The business plan is dated by the monthly financials included, and it is usually sent out in batches when it is being used as a financial tool, so don't make more copies than you need.

1. Computer Spreadsheets are Major Timesavers.

Financial data, more than any other type of information in your business plan, will become quickly dated. For that reason alone, keeping business plans on a computer with access to word processing and spreadsheet software is desired.

The other reason to put business plans on the computer is that the financial forecast section of the business plan is so easily modified in electronic spreadsheet form.

2. Few Forecasts Will Look Good a Year Later.

Looking at a five-year plan one year later often instills a great deal of humility regarding ability to forecast. Does this mean that forecasting and planning is a futile exercise for a small business? As far as accuracy is concerned, yes it does. But it is crucial to set goals. Otherwise, it is always a temptation to be reactive in a small business. Reacting to customer needs is a virtue. Reacting to financial needs is a vice, and the only way out of financial reaction is planning.

3. Financial Plans are General Directions, Not a Predestined Future.

Will planning rigidly determine the course of the business for the next five years? No. Will a plan guide the company toward long-term goals if it is done once a year? Yes, especially if the financial plan is integrated with a budget to carry it out. *A long-range financial plan receives its greatest justification from the fact that it is necessary to raise capital.* The financial plan is evidence of maturity and expertise that separate companies with professional management from mom-and-pop businesses.

4. Financial Planning Should Not be Delegated.

Don't delegate long-term financial planning to anyone who has not been with the company for a few years (or since inception in the case of a start-up). Investors are looking for the vision of the company's direction in the financial plan. An outside consultant or accountant cannot present that vision without a great deal of help from the general manager of the company.

A Business Plan Is Like a Company Resume

Having read Helena's guidelines, writing a business plan seemed like quite an undertaking to Jake, but at least he understood what needed to be done. As soon as he completed preparing it, Jake would be ready to seek formal sources of financing for Newcorp.

But Jake knew that even a successful business plan would not, of itself, acquire a dime for the company. What its achieves, at best, is to get the company an interview with a financing source. A business plan is much like a resume. Like a resume, it merely opens the door. It should stress accomplishment and how the company is going to make an investor some money. Marketing and sales forecasts must always be supported by convincing evidence. Expect that the interviewer will have read the marketing plan in great detail and will have done some research on his own. If his research conflicts, or if the business plan is shallow, it will severely damage your prospects of getting in the door.

Testing a Business Plan for Depth

One reliable method for testing how much someone knows is used by the CEO of a multi-billion-dollar international trading company. He picks an important area in a business plan and frames a question. After his first question is answered, he asks, "Why?" After the second question is answered he again asks, "Why?" If the third question can be answered with certainty, this CEO felt that the plan was well founded. He would reserve this line of questioning for one or two linch-pin areas in the plan. "Because" was not a sufficient answer, and this man became one of the wealthiest and most powerful men in his field by querying business people in this manner.

Answer the questions in the business plan guidelines three layers deep, particularly the questions related to the success or failure of the business. How well the plan was researched will be obvious.

In the next chapter, you will see Jake grapple with the many formal financing alternatives: venture capital, commercial bank financing, leasing versus purchase, and commercial finance-factoring. We will see why Jake decides on the latter alternative.

CHAPTER 7

Finding
Formal Sources
of Capital
for a
New Product
or Company

With his business plan in hand, Jake must now investigate and compare the various types of formal capital resources generally available to small business. Formal capital resources, like informal ones discussed in Chapter 5, are able to provide either debt (loans) or equity (investment) capital as appropriate. Jake will decide to use formal sources of debt to obtain more capital on the basis of the informal equity that he raised earlier (see Chapter 5). The capital provided by equity was used to purchase or produce inventory, accounts receivable, and fixed assets. Each of these categories of assets form collateral that can be used to permit borrowing.

Obtaining Venture Capital

Jake knew that the quantity of money needed for completing the capitalization process was larger than could be provided by his friends (the initial informal investors), and that he must try to obtain the money from the formal marketplace. He decided to begin by examining the process of obtaining professional venture capital.

Helena's network of friends proved a great asset to Jake. She set up an appointment with Roger Daily, president of a nearby venture capital company. The appointment was not to discuss an investment by Daily's firm in Newcorp, but to allow Jake an informal interview with a venture capitalist to find out how to proceed. Nonetheless, Helena told Jake to send Roger a business plan so that Roger's informal advice could be directed appropriately.

Too Many Passive Investors Are a Negative

When Jake arrived for his appointment, he thanked Roger for his time and he reviewed the financial history part of Newcorp's business plan. He mentioned that Newcorp had successfully raised one round of private investment. Then Jake explained that he had decided to seek capital from formal sources after he had initially considered making another private offering. He had realized that he would need more money than his group of friends could provide.

Disadvantages of Venture Capitalist Funding

Jake asked Roger if he would mind reviewing some of the pros and cons of professional venture capital. Roger began with some of the common negatives associated with professional venture capital—the stories that most small business people have heard who have ever asked about the wisdom of selling a part of their company to a venture capitalist.

The Probability of Funding Is Low

Low probability of obtaining funding is the rule, not the exception. Roger pointed to the pile of business plans on his desk. Venture capitalists receive far more business opportunities than they can invest in, so they have to select the ones that they think will be winners. Each venture capital company will have its own criteria. Some of them are obvious and advertised to the company seeking capital: regional preference, preferred size of investment, preferred type of business for investment, and so forth. Other criteria are not advertised: what experience is required of the management team; what rate of return is expected on the investment; whether or not the venture company is currently in the mode of looking for new investments, managing prior investments, or liquidating investments. The sum of all these factors was that only a very small percentage of those companies applying for venture capital would be successful in obtaining it.

Courting Venture Capital Chews Up Management Time

The venture capitalist asks for much more detailed information than does an informal investor. Gathering the information for a venture capital investor is extremely time consuming when the company can least afford to direct its management time to courting capital sources. Essentially, such clerical and planning activities defeat the major advantage of venture capital financing—saving time by going to a single known source of capital.

Venture Capitalists Often Demand Control

Professional venture capitalists frequently want both a larger share of the company and the right to purchase control, sometimes at inception. They often require that the company grow very rapidly and offer extraordinary rates of return.

Venture Capitalists Often Interfere with Management

Venture capital companies are well known for meddling with management. If they feel that the management is not capable of taking the company to its next stage of development, they will replace the founders with professional managers. If care is not exercised, the dilution experienced by the founders can be extreme, and they may be replaced.

Venture Capital Often Places a Company at Higher Risk

A major negative of involving professional venture capitalists, particularly the smaller or more aggressive ones, is that they have a requirement to turn their investment rather quickly. This can be a serious difficulty for a small company president working with real problems of trying to start a small business in a competitive and sometimes hostile environment. The rate of return requirement becomes more severe the higher interest rates become. And the higher the required rate of return, the higher the attendant risks. The risks result from pushing the company forward too rapidly rather than developing a strong market and normal rates of growth. The push for a quick return on investment has earned professional venture capital the unflattering nickname "vulture capitalist." The professional venture capitalist is not emotionally attached to his investments, and he will dump them if they are not performing. Being dumped is usually the kiss of death for a small company struggling to survive.

Now, like a good salesman he was, Roger closed with some of the major positives of professional venture capital.

Positive Aspects of Venture Capitalist Funding

Venture Capitalists Are Easy to Identify

Venture capital sources are easy to identify. Any public library or book store will have dozens of "how to do it" books on small business finance whose central contribution is to supply a list of addresses of professional venture capitalists along with the basic preferences of those sources.

Professionals Are Always Qualified to Invest

Professional venture capital, unlike many informal sources for investment funding, is always qualified. There is no risk to the small business owner that he or she will have sold stock to someone who will later sue under the guise of not having been properly qualified according to the SEC.

Professional venture capital is qualified in another very important way. They have money. Many of the solicitations of informal capital will end up in the hands of people who won't have the ready cash necessary to make an investment. If the venture capitalist takes time to look at a company, this is a fairly reliable indication that he is in an acquisition mode and that he will have the money to follow up with an investment if he likes the company.

Venture Capitalists Can Be Valuable Partners

Another positive of professional venture capitalists is that they have been though almost every mistake that can be made in developing a small business. Most of the good ones (and most of them are good or they aren't in business very long) will have gained a precious and very scarce commodity—wisdom. They will foresee problems that could catch inexperienced management by surprise. Of course, management won't always be interested in learning, but the professional venture capitalist is often a real gold mine of practical business knowledge. Before venture capitalists will make an investment in a company, they will become experts in the business. Indeed, they will often know a business better than its managers. "Why then," asked Jake, "wouldn't they go into that business instead of venture capital?" "My friend," said Roger, "going into your business is exactly what they are doing when they invest in you."

Venture Capitalists Are Experts in Going Public or Selling

The professional venture capitalist brings a unique financial skill to the table when he invests. In order for him to make a profit, he will have to liquidate his holding at some future time. This is often an opportunity for the founders to transforms their holdings from restricted stock to public stock. Suddenly the founders will find that they will be able to borrow on stock that was before totally illiquid. This can be quite advantageous if that stock has increased in value by virtue of having become a public company. The process of going public is discussed in Chapter 9. While going public is not a way to rapidly liquidate stock holdings for management, it can be successfully used to transform stock into collateral.

A professional venture capitalist can also help a company be acquired by a larger business. This, too, can be very lucrative to the founders. Most of the time the acquiring companies recognize that several transitional years will be necessary to absorb the new acquisition and that the old management will require strong incentives to stay. These deals are sometimes referred to as workouts. The founders will be given large incentives, in addition to the scheduled trade of their nonpublic stock for the public stock of the acquiring firm. Such incentives will be tied to performance, and they are designed to draw the little company into the structure of the larger company that has purchased it.

Professional Investors Increase the Chance of Success

In summary, one of the greatest advantages of being chosen by a professional venture capitalist is the knowledge that your company now has a much better chance of success in the vital area of turning your hard work into money at the end.

Jake thanked Roger for his time, and as he was driving home he realized for the first time why so many small high-technology companies requiring substantial start-up capital would choose to use a professional venture capitalist, often hiring a CFO if the CEO didn't have financial training.

Overview of Formal Sources of Debt

Jake's urgent requirement for capital was not likely to be met by the drawn-out process of obtaining professional venture capital, so he decided to look at professional debt sources next.

Unlike informal sources of debt, formal sources are much more particular about the way in which the repayment of debt is planned. For example, commercial banks loan on a medium-term basis against either (1) balance sheet ratios or (2) real estate and machinery collateral. Further, they insist that the source of repayment be clearly specified. Commercial banks must generally be quite conservative in their policy of loaning money. For instance, they will never provide capital for start-up enterprises. However, companies that do not fit such strict bank requirements should not overlook the option of higher-priced debt from commercial finance and factoring companies, which are asset-based (collateral) lenders. Since they are secured by assets in the case of default, such lenders have the latitude to be much more liberal in their lending policies than commercial banks.

The Small Business Administration (SBA) can also provide loans to small companies that are unable to meet the requirements of a bank. Special provisions are also made for minority and women-owned businesses, which may make the SBA the most favorable source of debt for companies with that type of ownership. It is a common misconception that the SBA loans only to minority-owned companies. But the vast majority of SBA loans are collateralized loans of last resort to small business regardless of their ownership. In order to obtain the SBA loan of last resort, the borrower must demonstrate that his company has been turned down several times by banks for conventional commercial loans.

Small Business Investment Corporations (SBICs) will be found among listings of professional venture capital sources. SBICs are often able to help a new company obtain an asset-based SBA loan. The SBA allows SBICs to issue debt several times greater than their capital. In addition to making traditional loans to businesses, SBICs are also allowed to produce other debt instruments such as convertible debentures (loans that are convertible to stock at the investor's option). Convertibles can be more attractive to investors than straight loans because of they permit participating in the profit growth of the business through conversion to stock.

Certain banks also serve as distributors of SBA guarantees. By this is meant that the bank actually makes the loan using its own deposits (like any commercial loan) but adds an SBA guarantee as further security. Most large commercial banks have full SBA departments and are authorized to commit SBA guarantees.

Jake will see that there is also a way to obtain capital equipment "off the balance sheet" through the leasing process—which means that the obligation does not appear as a direct liability.

Fact Sheet

As with all other means of financing, Jake had to prepare documentation to present Newcorp in a factually accurate and positive light. Before meeting with a vice president of his local branch bank for lunch to discuss a loan to meet the remainder of Newcorp's needs, Jake mailed a fact sheet for his loan request to the branch vice president. It contained brief answers to each of the following questions:

1. How much is being sought?
2. For how long?
3. At what range of rates?
4. What is the security for the loan?
5. What is the purpose for the loan?
6. Where are the funds for repayment coming from?
7. What are the backup plans for repayment?

By putting his request in writing, Jake enabled the vice president to understand Newcorp's requirements. Without such a fact sheet, much of the first meeting could be wasted by the bank trying to find what it was that Jake wanted. By sending the fact sheet ahead, the banker was prepared to size up Newcorp as a potential customer. For instance, if the amount being sought was larger than the local bank was accustomed to lending, no time at all would be wasted in discovering this fact over lunch. Similarly, each of the other questions would help the bank determine whether or not Newcorp would fit their portfolio.

Industry Average Comparisons

There was some additional homework that Helena suggested Jake do. Banks attempt to fit companies into industry groups in order to measure their relative performance. Many banks use *RMA Annual Statement Studies,* published by Robert Morris Associates, for this comparison. The studies include data on relative performance of companies by size (sales volume) and SIC (Standard Industry Code). By determining the closest SIC fit for Newcorp, and knowing the size of his company, Jake could look at the profile provided by Robert Morris against a ratio analysis of his own balance sheet.

If there were any anomalies in the ratios, they have to be explained. Most bankers listen closely to the explanation because they realize that industry performance ratings are gross averages hiding significant variation. The potential borrower's object is not to hide nonconforming areas, but to explain, logically, why such differences exist.

Modifying the Business Plan for Debt

The business plan that had been designed to present the company to equity investors had to be modified. First, the discussion of sale of stock would have to be changed to a discussion of borrowing. Second, since equity purchasers are more concerned with the appreciation of their stock value than the sources of debt repayment, sections had to be rewritten, and in some cases replanned, to sell a bank rather than a stockholder on the future of the business.

A Promising Project Might Not Be Bankable

At his lunch meeting with his banker, Ted, Jake was asked for a variety of basic documents that he was able to provide on the spot because he had planned ahead. Ted wanted the last three years of audited or reviewed financial statements (like an audit, a review is produced by a CPA, but it is less extensive and less expensive than a full audit), as well as the current financial statements of Newcorp. He wanted a cash flow projection and an inventory of fixed assets of the company. When Jake presented a business plan, Ted was pleased because many smaller companies were not so professionally prepared in their loan requests.

After several days had gone by, and Ted had made a presentation to the bank's loan committee, he stopped by Jake's office with a negative determination. Newcorp was too new. It didn't have the operating history or a proven cash flow history necessary to be bankable. (Bankable is a term meaning "having financial capacity sufficient to obtain a loan from a bank.")

SBA Loans

Jake asked Ted about an SBA loan as an alternative. Ted explained that his home office bank had an SBA department and that certain venture capital companies that were designated SBICs or SBIDCs (Small Business Industrial Development Corporations) could also make extended SBA-*guaranteed* loans. A bank's SBA department is often authorized to commit the SBA to guarantee the bank loan in cases where a company's cash flow and collateral base are not quite enough to qualify as nominally bankable. But, he warned, *loans that were clearly not bankable would not likely qualify for an SBA either. The guarantee is applicable in marginal situations only.*

Ted mentioned that if the new product had been produced under the auspices of Superdisk, rather than a new company, it might have been bankable with or without an SBA guarantee. Jake reflected silently that the bank would not have made the loan because Superdisk had had to reconstruct its credit ratings after a near meltdown. Another possibility, according to Ted, would have been to have Superdisk guarantee the Newcorp loan.

Ted also mentioned that, when Newcorp became operational and generated sales, some larger banks had the ability to loan against certain blue chip company receivables. His bank, being a smaller local branch of a larger bank, was unable to do this.

Jake persisted on the SBA option, indicating that he had heard that the SBA makes certain *direct* loans bypassing the bank, SBIC, or SBDIC altogether. Ted confirmed this, but said that such direct loans were usually reserved for companies owned by minorities or women, which was not Newcorp's profile.

Ted did, however, have one remaining suggestion. He gave Jake the phone number of Janet Maas, who was a loan officer at a commercial financing and factoring company.

Commercial Finance Companies

A commercial financing and factoring company was not a bank, Ted explained. They specialized in handling "second-tier" financing, usually companies that were not quite bankable. Ted felt that Newcorp had some special circumstances, particularly its forecast of significant receivables, that could form the basis of a factoring arrangement. Since Newcorp was projected to be significantly more profitable than Superdisk, Ted felt that the company could afford to pay the higher finance costs and save itself the time and dilution of trying to obtain professional venture capital.

Using a finance company does not destroy future bankability. After Newcorp had established a track record of cash flow and profitability for a year or two, Ted told Jake that the bank would be happy to reevaluate a new loan request, and that it would probably be accepted if the business evolved as Jake's plan for Newcorp indicated it would.

Finance Company Requirements

Jake set up an appointment with Janet Maas at Fleethill Capital Corporation. Jake provided a fact sheet ahead of time and had the basic shopping list of supporting documentation along with him. Fleethill had requirements similar to a bank, but they were much more centered upon asset collateral than cash flow. The cash flow still had to be there because finance companies, contrary to common mythology, do not want to have to foreclose and sell the collateral. Rather, they are simply in the business of making and managing riskier loans at a higher interest rate.

The meeting with Janet went well. Because Newcorp was a new customer, Fleethill was willing to loan only up to 70% on approved receivables so long as they fit within rules of concentration (no more than 20% of receivables located with a single customer) and excluding government accounts. Janet wanted to do a credit check on each of his customers in order to determine whether or not they were a good enough credit risk for factoring. (Receivable financing involves the factor actually purchasing the receivable from Newcorp, and requires notification of the payer to remit the proceeds directly to the factor and allow factor endorsement of checks in some cases.) There were ways in which to factor government accounts, but each had to be approved on a per contract basis, since the government would not forward its checks to the Fleethill account without elaborate documentation.

The only problem with the factoring arrangement that Jake could see was that they were coming up substantially short of the total amount of funds that he needed. Jake had assumed that 80% of all his receivables would be factored while, in reality, only 70% of selected receivables could be used. Janet suggested that Fleethill was also in the business of loaning on property and equipment, and that the machinery at Newcorp might form the basis for a longer-term loan. Janet advocated the longer-term loan not only from Fleethill's self-interest, but from the point of view that it would improve the projected current ratio of Newcorp during its early developmental stages. Janet told Jake the loan amount would include provisions for working capital as well as equipment. Typically the equipment portion of the loan package will be at 60% of the established market value in the used equipment market.

Jake left the Fleethill office somewhat heartened at the prospect of immediate funding, but he wanted to examine one more option before making a final decision.

Leasing *vs.* Purchasing and Borrowing

Jake realized he could purchase new equipment with the investment money he had raised, and leverage those purchases by borrowing back a percentage of the purchase price from the finance company. Helena advised that they first look into leasing. Typically leasing is available only on new equipment, but the full value of the equipment can be financed rather than the partial percentage allowed by borrowing back on the purchases from the finance company.

Helena noted that the lease rates could be analyzed with a simple business calculator to determine the equivalent to interest being paid for the lease. Often, the lease rate is higher than the interest rate charged by a finance company, but a lease is usually much easier for a new company to acquire than any type of loan.

A financial consultant such as Helena could easily produce a lease-purchase analysis for Jake, and he would be well advised to lease any equipment his company really required.

Finance Company's Audit

After looking at his alternatives, Jake realized that his aversion to finance company funding was founded upon old myths, and that

Fleethill was an excellent source of capital for his new and rapidly growing company.

For the next few weeks, Fleethill's people practically lived at Newcorp. They independently audited the financials, they counted and valued the inventory, and they appraised the property and machines that were being offered as collateral for the long term loan. They acted like someone who was planning to become a business partner—not at all like the detached treatment Jake had come to expect from the bank.

At the end of their research, Fleethill presented a package to Jake that met all his requirements for Newcorp. All that remained was to make the business plan happen as projected, and then Newcorp could migrate back to the less-expensive and less-intrusive relation with the bank. In the meanwhile, much like a professional venture capitalist, Fleethill would be an excellent financial partner because they were watching the performance of Newcorp very closely. If any of the multitude of ratios used by Fleethill indicated that Newcorp was out of the bounds of their agreement, funds could be withheld until the problem was solved and Newcorp was returned to conformance.

Valuing and Selling a Small Company Using a Business Broker

Some years have passed, Newcorp has been successfully merged with Superdisk, and Superdisk has indeed lived out a full life. Jake successfully curbed cash meltdown, reestablished permanent controls, restored profitability by reshuffling the product mix, and successfully launched a new product with the help of founder's capital and a factor-financing sources. Jake now wonders if his dreams of founding and maturing his product idea can be monetized. He is considering selling and comfortably retiring on the proceeds, but wonders how to proceed.

This chapter and the next present simple procedures and practices on valuing and selling the Superdisk enterprise. Chapter 8 details how a small business broker can help Jake walk away from the firm following a real estate closing procedure with a large chunk of cash as down payment and a handsome annuity on a note secured by the assets of the company. Chapter 9 describes the process of Superdisk's alternative—going public.

The decision to sell out or go public rests on Jake's intentions. If it is time to personally get out, it is time to sell out. If Jake wants to continue in the company but worries about how his heirs would liquidate should something happen to him, he might consider going public to gradually give liquidity to his shares in the company. His heirs can simply sell the shares at his demise.

The Business Broker

Sales of businesses are normally handled by specialized business brokers. These men and women possess regular real estate licenses but come from different backgrounds than the typical residential sales agent. Competent business brokers are specialists from corporate backgrounds, often from finance or accounting, and therefore are comfortable with balance sheets and appraisal techniques. Such knowledge is indispensable. Using its expertise, an East Coast business brokerage firm sells 80% to 95% of its listing right at the listed price, and because of careful screening, it successfully sells about 75% of all listings accepted.

Jake should never list his business with a residential or real estate broker who places the business in multiple listing. Selling a business is a highly confidential matter and cannot be indiscreetly publicized for fear of jeopardizing the existing customer base. Therefore it is almost mandatory to use a business brokerage firm that employs full-time professionals who only sell businesses. The expertise of the broker is critical to these transactions.

There *is* a point when a broker is not the best choice. Generally if the selling price of a company reached $1 to 1.5 million, it should be handled by an investment banker rather than a business broker (although some business brokers can handle sales of this size.) The investment banker can either arrange a private placement, assist in the sale to a larger firm, or take the company public.

Pricing Considerations

Pricing varies with the type of business. For the example of a light manufacturer such as Superdisk, the price is comprised of the value of inventory, fixed assets, and goodwill. What the buyer always asks is whether he or she can start from scratch and avoid paying extra for goodwill. For an established business to sell for more than the basic asset value (*i.e.,* include goodwill), the business broker must be able to establish a price that 1) provides for profit returns sufficient to cover a normal return on the buyer's invested capital, 2) provides for a salary for the buyer if he participates in the business (or for a manager if absentee owned), and 3) provides at least a modest residual profit.

Down Payments

Sellers normally require a down payment of at least the inventory plus equipment, with goodwill being carried back by the seller as a loan to the buyer. Such a method is a protection for both the buyer and the seller. For example, were the buyer to put down only one-half the inventory, he could easily strip the business of inventory, fixed assets, and real estate, sell them and default on his agreement with the seller, in effect, raiding the company's assets without any intention of long-run operations for profit.

At the other extreme is the buyer who puts all cash down, including the goodwill (intangible assets.) He is at risk if the business does not produce earnings claimed by the seller (perhaps because the seller was indispensable to the business). By asking the seller to carry a note for the goodwill, the buyer is saying he will pay if the profits (stemming from the goodwill) are realized; otherwise he will simply sell off inventory and equipment, recoup his down payment, and return the business to the seller.

Rule-of-Thumb Valuation Method

The rule-of-thumb method is one way a broker values a business for sale. For example, one western brokerage firm sets a price at inventory plus "adjusted fixed assets" (including land and buildings) plus the equivalent of one year's "discretionary income" as goodwill. (All terms are defined in the example below.)

In a typical example of the rule-of-thumb method, assume

Superdisk has inventory of $40,000, depreciated fixed assets of $50,000, accumulated depreciation over the years of $10,000, and has after-tax profits of $20,000. The seller also receives a salary of $40,000, has a free car and health/life insurance worth $18,000 per year, and has an annual bonus of $6,000.

What is the value of the business and what should the down payment be? The value of land, buildings, and equipment under the rule-of-thumb method of $50,000 plus $5,000 (which is a 50% add back of accumulated depreciation). The value of goodwill, at $84,000, is based on discretionary income, which is defined as the sum of $20,000 profits, $40,000 salary, $18,000 perks, and a $6000 bonus. Finally, adding in inventory, and assuming a 10% brokerage commission, the following list price is placed on the business:

Inventory	$40,000	
Adjusted fixed assets	55,000	($50,000 plus half of $10,000)
Goodwill	84,000	
Broker's commission at 10%	18,000	
Total List Price	$197,000	

Long-Form Valuation Method

An alternative valuation method, called the long-form method, was adapted from *Inc.* magazine (July, 1982). It has been used successfully by at least one major firm for valuing a going concern. The method involves seven steps, described below.

Step 1: Determining Stabilized Income

Step 1 establishes a stabilized income. The premise is that profits from last year might not apply next year. Also, certain

TABLE 8–1

Calculating Stabilized Income

	Last 12 Months		(Stabilized Next 12 Months)	
Sales (1)	$650,000	100.0%	$700,000	100.0%
Cost of goods (2)	($197,600)	30.4	($212,800)	30.4
Operating labor (3)	($187,000)	28.8	($201,600)	28.8
Gross profit (3)	$265,400	40.8	$285,600	40.8
Sales expense (4)	($86,750)	13.3	($92,400)	13.2
Administrative expense (4)	($52,650)	8.1	($42,000)	6.0
Executive salaries (3)	($40,000)	6.2	($49,000)	7.0
Replacement fund (5)	($11,700)	1.8	($21,000)	3.0
Maintenance & repairs (4)	($5,200)	0.8	($7,000)	1.0
Unclassified (4)	($5,200)	0.8	($7,000)	1.0
Total overhead expense	($201,500)	31.0	($218,400)	31.2
Indicated pretax profit	$63,900	9.8	$67,200	9.6

Assumptions:
(1) Sales will increase at inflation rate assumed to be 7.7%
(2) Operating cost will remain at constant percentages.
(3) Executive (owner) salary should be increased by $9,000 to reflect current salaries offered in comparable businesses.
(4) Minor adjustments were made through a detailed analysis of each line item or expense and reflect best estimates.
(5) Replacement fund of $21,000 will be substituted for depreciation expense. This is ample to replace assets as they wear out.

accounting techniques employed to avoid taxes can hide real earnings. Finally, nonrecurring expenses and revenues must be removed from consideration. Table 8–1 shows the calculation. Notice the assumptions at the bottom of the table.

Based upon past performance, sales in this example are expected to rise 7.7% to $700,000 next year. Other expense items rise at the same percentage of sales as last year. Notice the replacement fund. This is analogous to depreciation of equipment, but it is adjusted to provide a fund for full replacement of equipment when it wears out. Notice also the executive salaries, which are increased beyond what the seller currently receives to reflect current employment market conditions (perhaps the buyer will work in the business, in which case he or she participates in executive salaries). Overall, stabilized income is determined to be $67,200.

Step 2: Valuing Tangible Assets

Step 2 establishes the value of tangible assets. An example for a hypothetical case is shown below. These figures would normally be derived from buyer estimations or through direct appraisal.

Value of Tangible Assets

Land	$20,000
Buildings	$120,000
Inventory	$60,000
Equipment	$60,000
Value of assets acquired	$260,000
Plus working capital required	$40,000
Total Assets	$300,000

Step 3: Calculating Cost of Money

In Step 3 the "cost of money" is computed. This is analogous to a basic return for investing. However, because this percentage must be stable (and cannot fluctuate with interest rates), the inflation rate plus 4 percentage points is established as the cost of money.

The inflation rate is published quarterly and is therefore more stable than the prime rate, which can change frequently and produce wild gyrations in the business valuation. In practice, 4 percentage points have been a rule-of-thumb risk premium over the riskless inflation rate.

The cost of money at 12% (inflation of 8% plus 4 points) of total assets ($300,000 from Table 8–2) is $36,000:

Cost of Money

Total assets	$300,000
Underlying interest rate	12%
Cost of money (.12 × $300,000)	$36,000

Step 4: Calculating Excess Earnings

Stabilized earnings of $67,200 (from Table 8–1) minus the cost of money of $36,000 produces "excess earnings" of $31,200:

Excess Earnings

Stabilized earnings	$67,200
Cost of money	($36,000)
Excess earnings	$31,200

Step 5: Excess Earnings Multiple

Value is normally related to some multiple of earnings. Step 5 computes an excess earning multiple based upon a rating scale illustrated in Table 8–2. Notice the several rating categories from which numbers applicable to the listed business are chosen. In this case the final earnings multiple of 3.9 is the arithmetic average of all the ratings assigned.

TABLE 8–2

Calculating the Excess Earnings Multiple

Key to Rating Scale

Risk rating (from 0 to 6)

0 = Continuity of income at risk

3 = Steady income likely

6 = Growing income assured

Company rating (from 0 to 6)

0 = Recent start-up, not established

3 = Well established with satisfactory environment

6 = Long record of sound operation with outstanding reputation

Competitive rating (from 0 to 6)

0 = Highly competitive in unstable market

3 = Normal competitive conditions

6 = Little competition in market, high cost of entry for new competition

Company growth rating (from 0 to 6)

0 = Business has been declining

3 = Steady growth, slightly faster than inflation rate

6 = Dynamic growth rate

Industry rating (from 0 to 6)

0 = Declining industry

3 = Industry growing somewhat faster than inflation

6 = Dynamic industry, rapid growth likely

Desirability rating (from 0 to 6)

0 = No status, rough or dirty work

3 = Respected business in satisfactory environment

6 = Challenging business in attractive environment

Sample Rating Formula

Risk	4.0
Competitive situation	3.0
Industry	3.5
Company	5.0
Company growth	4.0
Desirability	4.0
Total	23.5
Excess earnings multiple (Total ÷ 6)	3.9

Step 6: Valuing Excess Earnings

In the next step, excess earnings of $31,200 (see Step 4) are multiplied by the earnings multiplier of 3.9 to produce a "market value of excess earnings" of $121,680. This is the value of goodwill and is the premium charged over basic assets because the company is an established enterprise.

Valuing Excess Earnings

Excess earnings	$31,200
Multiple	×3.9
Value of excess earnings	$121,680

Step 7: Computing the Listing Price

Finally, the listing price of $381,680 is the sum of $260,000 inventory, equipment, and other acquired assets (see Step 2) plus the $121,680 value of goodwill. (See Step 6). In this example, after the purchase the buyer should also be prepared to add about $40,000 for working capital to the business.

Total Business Value

Value of assets acquired	$260,000
Value of excess earnings	$121,680
Total business listing value	$381,680

Frequently the actual listing price will be stated as "$321,680 plus inventory at closing," since inventory fluctuates.

Valuation Adjusted to Performance

The two methods of fixed valuation illustrated above are generally applicable to most businesses. One variant of these methods involves what is called the "earnout," or "valuation adjusted to performance." Under an earnout, a business purchased for $300,000 might have a provisional purchase price of $225,000 and graduate up to the full $300,000 (or more because the seller takes risk) only if certain stipulated sales materialize; otherwise, perhaps after four to five years, the $225,000 becomes the final price. This form is common when purchasing complex businesses such as manufacturing companies.

Other Methods of Valuation

In highly specialized businesses, often simple multiples suffice for establishing the sale price. For example, an accounting company in the southwest would currently be valued at one times gross receipts, or so much per account acquired by the purchaser. A motel in the northeast would be worth about three times annual room gross income. Mature manufacturing companies are sometimes valued (excluding real estate) at one time gross receipts for the immediately prior year.

In terms of down payment, a service business might require one third down, with a carryback by the seller for three to seven years, depending upon the profitability of the enterprise.

Industry-specific guides to value are available from specific trade journals and national trade associations.

Skim Not Valued

In valuing a company, the broker will take great care so as not to count as profits those skimmed off the top before taxable income is calculated. Owners of cash businesses such as laundromats, bars, and liquor stores typically skim off the top to save on taxes. Brokers will, therefore, recommend an average of the last three to five years of income tax statements be used for determination of income to assess how much goodwill to list for. Brokers will not take the seller's word that a company is making more than income reported for tax, because there is no way to verify such illegal skim.

Covenant Not to Compete

Buyers typically require that the seller not set up a similar business within the same county, or within five to fifty miles, for a period of three to five years (seven years maximum). This is necessary to protect the business sold from being pirated by the seller, who might set up across the street and draw away all his old customers.

Buyers should require (with the seller's formal agreement) that the covenant include a dollar figure equal to 50% of the amount of goodwill. This value can be amortized over five years for tax purposes, thereby effectively making the government subsidize the purchase price through the tax deduction. For example, if a $200,000 sale includes $100,000 in goodwill, $50,000 could be amortized over five years, or $10,000 per year. For a small firm with a subchapter S tax rate of 28%, these deductions are worth $2,800 per year of actual tax rebate to the buyer.

Owner Financing

In order to make the deal feasible to the buyer, the seller is usually asked to take back a note. To "take back" or to "carry back" simply means that the seller loans some of the sale price to the buyer. The interest rate on the carryback should be concessionary as an incentive to the buyer. Typically, the rate is prime + 1%.

The maturity of the carryback is usually sufficiently long term to allow the buyer to service the seller loan and still obtain a decent return on his down payment plus imputed salary. Thus, the carryback on a company that is not particularly profitable might stretch out longer than one with more immediate earning power.

Fees

Brokerage fees exceed those for residential sales, reflecting the expertise required. Some eastern firms use a sliding scale that includes 10% for the first $500,000 of sale price, 7% for the next $500,000, and continues to slide down to 1% for any amount over $5,000,000. Certain western brokerages quote 12% on the first $150,000, 10% on $500,000, and for listings over $1 million they charge on a 5–4–3–2–1 sliding scale, i.e., 5% for the first million, 4% for the second million, and so on. Using the 5–4–3–2–1 method, a $2 million listing would cost the seller a 9% commission.

A "Good" Listing

Dealing knowledgeably with a business broker can spare Jake the disappointment of a mispriced business that never sells. A good business will have been established for three to five years, will have a track record of good cash flows, and will be priced at a realistic amount. Goodwill priced at more than two times cash flow will generally not work financially for the buyer, and, as a result, the buyer will default and return the business to the seller. At that point, the business is typically in much worse shape than when originally sold.

While the thought of selling Superdisk and walking away with the money appealed to Jake's dreams of independence, he knew he loved his work as much as any other recreation he could imagine. So, he decided to examine the possibility of an initial public offering (IPO) of stock for Superdisk. In an initial public offering, his stock sale would be restricted to small portions for a long period of time, but he could begin to borrow on it if the firm was well managed. And it would be a great challenge to continue growing Superdisk with the funds from the IPO.

Going Public
or
Being Acquired

Chapter 9 reviews the opportunities and difficulties of a public offering *vs.* private sale. These methods of raising capital and gaining liquidity are contrasted with bank financing and venture capital sources. As will be shown, with the exception of a corporate sellout, these financial mediums are used more for raising capital for growth than as a means of establishing value for liquidity purposes.

Considerations in Going Public

Going Public Is Not Selling Out

Going public is not a means of selling out and retiring. Investors in newly public companies are looking for the presence of a solid management team and established control systems. The corporation that goes public has the intention of growing and fully exploiting its products. If the original management team cannot meet these conditions, and often they cannot, they must be replaced, usually shortly after going public. More often than not, a team of successful entrepreneurs are not skilled managers of a growing business. The skills necessary to start a company are quite different than those required to manage it after it is a going concern. When a company matures to the stage of going public, it is assumed that it is sufficiently mature to undergo the transition to new management successfully. Since the entrepreneural management team owns large amounts of stock, they can be counted upon to support the transition to professional management as being in their own interest financially.

SEC Restricts Sales of Personal Stock

If Jake wants to cash out, going public is not the way to do it because he will be restricted in how much of his stock he can sell, whether or not he is allowed to remain on the management team. Rule 144 of the Securities and Exchange Commission specifically applies to insiders who want to take their company public and immediately dump personal shares on the market. Generally the insider can sell only 1% of the average monthly trading volume, and then only upon prior notification of his intention to do so through the SEC. At this rate, the sale of a 49% stake (assuming Jake retains control with 51%) would take over twelve years. The new rules on insider trading are intended to protect investors, who view insider selling as an indication that management does not have faith in the long-term prospects of the company.

In addition to the SEC restrictions on stock trade, the underwriter (investment banker) who takes the company public will often restrict the sale of any insider stock for a period of several years as part of the underwriting agreement. The purpose of such additional restrictions is to help sustain the market, particularly in penny issues.

A Public Offering Costs Time and Money

Another consideration in making a public offering is its expense. For a $3 to $5 million public offering, Jake can plan on about 12% to 15% in costs of making the offering due to brokerage, financial public relations, audit, printing, due diligence, and legal fees. On the penny stock market, a $6 million issue might net only slightly more than $5 million in proceeds to the issuing company.

Another important factor influencing the decision to go public is that a substantial management time is required to promote the stock prior to the formal underwriting. The CEO must go on the road to tout the company to brokers and investors in various parts of the country, neglecting corporate operations for four to six months. Furthermore, employees distracted from their jobs by the excitement of following the hourly movement of a newly issued stock are inefficient, and productivity can drop.

Reporting Requirements

Jake also had to consider the reporting requirements on a full public offering, which are significant. The 10K report, required by the SEC, is an extension of the annual report and involves the recitation of personal as well as corporate activities. For example, perks such as a car, free insurance, stock options, club memberships, and travel, which Jake might have routinely taken from the private business, now must be fully reported. In addition, a 10Q report, which is an abbreviated 10K report, must be filed quarterly. If the company does not already employ a chief financial officer, it will have to hire one before going public, and the CFO will spend as much as one fourth of his time producing the 10K and 10Q reports on an ongoing basis.

Overall, because of underwriting costs and reporting requirements, penny stock underwriters generally will not agree to take a company public if the equity issue is less than $4 to $5 million. The more reputable underwriters will insist on sales of $15 to $20 million per year and initial offerings above $7 million.

The Stockholder Is King

Going public will require Jake to reorient himself toward serving the stockholder, even if he retains majority control (which is unlikely). Jake will be forced to think in terms of very short-term performance and often bypass projects with medium-term potential that require the absorption of short-term losses.

Do You Need the Cash?

A final consideration in justifying an initial public offering is having a valid business need for all the cash generated. Cash is usually needed to capitalize future growth—the vehicle for appreciation of the stock. If a company does not relish the added stress of rapid growth, then a public offering is definitely a wrong step.

Advantages of Going Public

Going public early can provide needed growth capital not generally available from other sources. A public offering in the penny stock market is sometimes possible even before becoming profitable. In this regard, it has been estimated that as much as $1 to $5 in value could be raised in a public offering for every $1 in sales, where product growth prospects are extremely strong. For mature products, the ratio of stock price per share to sales per share may be a low as 1:1.

In contrast with bank financing and venture capitalist funding, an advantage of a public offering is that a company can do whatever it wants with the proceeds, subject to public disclosure of general plans for their use.

A further advantage of a public offering is that a company can generally get more value for the company than it can through an acquisition by another company or through other sources. The reason for this is that the public investor must pay a premium for the privilege of being able to rapidly buy and sell small quantities of ownership. In contrast, a corporate acquirer buys at a lower price to compensate for the risk of having to wait months or years to sell, perhaps in a declining market, when the company might be reporting losses. In essence, the corporate acquisition price is a wholesale price, while the public pays a retail price.

Finally, equity rather than debt is actually cheaper since no interest is paid on stock (generally dividends are not paid until the firm becomes seasoned) and equity never is repaid. Therefore, a stock offering protects the corporate income from interest expense and preserves its cash flow.

Over-the-Counter (OTC) Market

A private company with an established product, a good management team, and a management information system in place, could be a candidate for underwriting in the OTC market. A firm in this category usually has a banking relationship for short-term working capital but does not have the capital to grow rapidly enough to grab available market share. If it can obtain an underwriter (and this is a function of the market for initial public offerings, or IPOs, more than the strength of the company or its prospects), it may attempt an IPO in the OTC.

Penny Stock Market

The penny stock market is a subset of the OTC market and it refers, strictly speaking, to stocks issued or trading for less than a dollar. Since many new issues quickly sink to half or a third of their issue price, new issues offered at less than $3 are also referred to as penny issues. By far, the greatest majority of OTC trading is for stocks worth more than $1 and traded on the national over-the-counter (NASDAQ) exchange. Some OTC trading is also done on the regional exchanges.

Generally, penny stock issues are considered more speculative than stocks of companies trading at several dollars or more. Due to the very small float ("float," in the context of stock issues, is the amount of stock able to be traded in the marketplace), the price of penny stock issues can fluctuate more rapidly than large company issues having large floats.

Because the speculative penny market is primarily bought by the small investor who is not able to evaluate its risks, the SEC and some states have literally tried to shut down this market. These moves have been strongly resisted by "free market" advocates as well as the affected underwriters. Of significant impact is the recent SEC effort to restrict cold calling, a primary method of marketing pennies by small brokerages that do not have the resources of the national and multinational brokers.

At its best, the penny market has been a bulwark of the American economic system—a way to level the playing field and allow small business to access enough fairly priced capital to compete in niches uneconomic for big companies to pursue. Important products that have greatly improved the productivity of American business—such the automobile, photocopiers, and a host of software products—have all emerged from small companies.

At its worst, the penny market is fraudulent—a home for fast buck operators preying upon the unwary.

A company considering a penny stock offering, and often this is the only option open to small companies, should carefully inspect its underwriter. Call the SEC and ask if there have ever been any irregularities with the underwriter and if they have any record of past or pending litigation against the underwriter. The company should also call the CEO of the last several companies brought public by the underwriter to obtain an opinion. These simple and brief due diligence checks will quickly reveal if a penny stock under-writer is trustworthy.

Mezzanine Financing

In the instance where a company is insufficiently developed to go public but is definitely planning to go public when it is able, an investment banker might suggest a two-year bond or preferred stock issue to be repaid at maturity by a common stock issue. This in between, or "mezzinine," financing gives the company growth capital now while preparing for the public offering.

In order to market the bonds, warrants (separate certificates guarantee stock purchase at a fixed price) are sometimes attached as marketing incentives to sell the issue.

Venture Capital Financing Precedes IPO

The timing for an IPO is often not in the hands of the company making the offer; rather it is a function of the market for new issues. The penny market is even more fickle than the market for new OTC issues in general. For this reason, IPOs have become more of a vehicle for venture capitalists to divest themselves of a company when they have made a profit. The venture capitalist makes a long-term investment and can generally afford to hold until the market for IPOs is favorable.

In contrast, an independent company seeking capitalization to meet its business requirements can't wait for the IPO market to bloom. Unless a small company is very fortunate, it is unlikely that the timing of its offering will coincide with a good stock market climate. Therefore, the most likely path for a small company wanting funds for growth is first to obtain professional venture capital, and sometime thereafter to make an initial public offering.

Being Acquired by a Larger Company

Because access to public markets is often limited, private companies often consider selling out to a larger company interested in its technology or potential. This is a means of selling out and walking away, although the purchaser will frequently ask the seller to stay on as a consultant to smooth over the transition to new management.

Generally Jake will not receive as much in proceeds under a sellout compared with going public because the corporate buyer is usually represented by sharp negotiators who are looking for a bargain while acquiring new technology or a promising product. A corporate buyer expects a wholesale price for his wholesale purchase.

If there is a management team in place, golden parachutes (big compensation for early retirement) and other incentives are sometimes utilized to make room for new management from the acquiring firm. Middle management of the acquired firm, however, will often lose their jobs with modest severance pay packages, and top management which hangs on can expect the same treatment when the acquiring firm thinks its utility is ended.

If Jake sells out to a corporation, he will probably get some cash plus stock in the acquiring corporation. This means that he must carefully evaluate the financial viability and future prospects of the purchasing company, especially if its shares are not yet publicly traded, (meaning that Jake will have to hold them for some time). Incidentally, if Jake were to take all stock, it would be tax free and subject to taxation only upon his subsequent sale of shares of the larger company.

Setting a Price for Stock

While there are many methods of valuing a firm for going public, (that is, establishing a price for the stock to be offered), investment bankers cite three that are most common, listed in the order of preference: the price-earnings (P/E) method, the market-capital-to-total-sales-ratio method, and the price-to-book-value-ratio method. These three methods involve comparing Superdisk with a similar publicly traded firm to come up with a stock price.

Price-Earnings Method

Assume that ABC Company is listed on the American Stock Exchange, has a P/E ratio of 10:1, a stock priced at $20, and an earnings per share of $2. These measures of performance are available in the reference section of most libraries.

To compare ABC with Superdisk, assume Jake has estimated that 400,000 private shares will be outstanding after the new share issue and that after-tax earnings are $96,109. Jake calculates an earnings per share of $0.24 ($96,109 ÷ 400,000 shares). Since the stock of ABC Company trades at ten times earnings, then the issue price of Superdisk stock should be $2.40 (10 × $0.24). In actual practice, the number of shares of the IPO will be varied to produce a valuation within a range that will sell.

Market-Capital-to-Total-Sales-Ratio Method

Market capitalization for a public company is the share price times the number of common shares outstanding. For example, if ABC Company has a share price of $20 with 500,000 shares outstanding, then the market capitalization is $10 million. If total product sales are $30 million, then the ratio for ABC is 0.33 ($10 million capital ÷ $30 million total sales).

If product sales of Superdisk are $3,777,564, then market capitalization is calculated to be $1,246,596 (0.33 × $3,777,564). If 400,000 shares are expected to be issued, then the share price would be $3.12 ($1,246,596 ÷ 400,000 shares).

Price-to-Book-Value-Ratio Method

If ABC Company has a share price of $20 and a book value of $10 per share, then the price-to-book ratio is 2.0. Assuming Superdisk has a net worth of $957,776 and anticipates having 400,000 shares after the new share issue, then the book value per share is $2.39. Using the ratio for ABC Company, Superdisk should issue shares at $4.78 (2.0 × $2.39).

Comparing the three methods, Jake might estimate that Superdisk should issue common stock at a price of $3.44, the average of the three prices calculated above. Because Superdisk is new to the market, it would probably be priced at $3.00.

A second example is given using for comparison a computer peripheral company, Seagate Technology, traded OTC. Financial information for this company, taken from Value Line Investors Services (available in libraries), is shown in Table 9–1.

Using the P/E method, Superdisk stock should be issued at $3.07 per share (12.8 × $0.24).

Using the ratio of market capital to sales, first calculate that ratio for Seagate: $967.5 million ÷ $1,266 million = 0.764. Applying this ratio to Superdisk, and assuming sales of $3,778,000, market value is $2,886,392 (market value ÷ $3,778,000 = 0.764). With

TABLE 9–1

Seagate Technology Compared to Superdisk

	Seagate Technology Prior Year	Superdisk Current Year
Price-earnings ratio	12.8	
Book value per share	$8.89	$2.39
Shares outstanding	49,090,000	400,000
Earnings per share	$1.54	$0.24
Stock price	$19.71	
Market capitalization	$967,500,000	
Gross Sales	$1,266,000,000	$3,778,000

400,000 shares to be outstanding, Superdisk should trade at $7.22 per share ($2,886,392 ÷ 400,000 shares).

Using the ratio of price to book value, Seagate has a market-to-book ratio of 2.22 ($19.71 ÷ $8.89). Applying this ratio to Superdisk, we find the firm should issue stock at $5.31 (stock price ÷ $2.39 = 2.22).

Superdisk could average the three prices to obtain $5.20 per share. A similar calculation can be made by any business owner contemplating going public.

We leave Jake much happier than we found him. At the beginning of the narrative he was struggling to survive. At the end he is trying to decide between several attractive options.

Postscript

Jake's hypothetical return from a near meltdown can't match the precise experience of every small business that has found itself in trouble. Not everyone has a Newcorp waiting to become an instant success and save the company. Most can't conceive of having the time to start a second company while reconstructing the first company was barely begun. Everyone doesn't have a friend as knowledgeable as Helena.

These and other differences should not obscure the fact that solutions to many of the most common financial shortcomings of small businesses are covered here in such a way that a determined owner will be able to help himself. Finance is not something that just happens to a small business. The resourceful person has a surprisingly large number of ways to survive financially if he or she is willing to do the analytical work, the planning, the formatting, and presentation required to obtain financial banking.

Appendix

Sample Offering
Memorandum
for Newcorp, Inc.

The following pages contain the text of a sample offering memorandum required by the Securities and Exchange Commission and various state securities departments. The sample is structured for the State of California. Each state has different requirements, of which the offering memorandum is only one. You are urged to seek professional legal help if you decide to make an offering of stock. A formal offering memorandum is often not required for the sale of stock to founders and is usually not required for the sale of stock to venture capitalists. But it *is* required for all new stock issues sold to the public, and it may be a wise move even for sale of stock to founders in case of future misunderstandings or disagreements.

NEWCORP, INC.
PRIVATE PLACEMENT
MEMORANDUM
OFFERING OF COMMON STOCK
APRIL 1, 1991

This memorandum contains information that is sensitive to New-corp, Inc. Potential investors agree not to disclose such information without permission of Newcorp. The material herein shall not be duplicated.

Memorandum Number: _____

This copy assigned to: _____

TABLE OF CONTENTS

100,000 COMMON SHARES
4 UNITS OF 25,000 SHARES EACH ($25,000 PURCHASE)
NEWCORP, INC.
COMMON STOCK

There is not now nor has there previously been any market for the shares of Newcorp, Inc. (the "Company"). No assurance can be given that a trading market will develop at any time after this Offering or, if such a market does develop, that it will be sustained.

AN INVESTMENT IN THE COMPANY'S SHARES INVOLVES A HIGH DEGREE OF RISK AND SHARES SHOULD BE PURCHASED ONLY BY PERSONS WHO CAN AFFORD THE RISK OF LOSS OF THEIR ENTIRE INVESTMENT. SEE SECTION 4, RISK FACTORS.

THESE SECURITIES HAVE NOT BEEN APPROVED OR DISAPPROVED BY THE SECURITIES AND EXCHANGE COMMISSION, NOR HAS THE SECURITIES AND EXCHANGE COMMISSION PASSED UPON THE ACCURACY OR ADEQUACY OF THIS MEMORANDUM. NO STATE REGISTRATION OF THESE SECURITIES HAS BEEN SOUGHT OR OBTAINED, AND NO STATE AGENCY HAS REVIEWED, APPROVED, DISAPPROVED, OR PASSED UPON THESE SECURITIES OR THIS MEMORANDUM. ANY REPRESENTATION TO THE CONTRARY IS A CRIMINAL OFFENSE.

Price to Investors	Proceeds to Company
$1.00 per share	$1.00 per share
$1,000,000.00	$1,000,000.00

COMMON STOCK CURRENTLY OUTSTANDING

There is currently one class of common stock issued and outstanding. All common stock is currently owned by Jake Z. Jones as shown in Section 14, Principal Stockholders.

THIS MEMORANDUM DOES NOT CONSTITUTE AN OFFER TO ANY PERSON IN ANY JURISDICTION WHERE SUCH AN OFFER WOULD BE UNLAWFUL. NO PERSON HAS BEEN AUTHORIZED TO GIVE ANY INFORMATION OR TO MAKE ANY REPRESENTATIONS OTHER THAN THOSE CONTAINED IN THIS MEMORANDUM. ANY SUCH OTHER INFORMATION OR REPRESENTATIONS, IF MADE OR GIVEN, MUST NOT BE RELIED UPON BY THE RECIPIENT OR HIS REPRESENTATIVE AS HAVING BEEN AUTHORIZED BY THE COMPANY. THE DELIVERY OF THIS MEMORANDUM AT ANY TIME DOES NOT IMPLY THAT THE INFORMATION HEREIN IS CORRECT AS OF ANY TIME SUBSEQUENT TO ITS DATE. THESE SECURITIES ARE OFFERED SUBJECT TO PRIOR SALE, REJECTION OF ANY OFFER TO PURCHASE FOR ANY REASON, AND TO WITHDRAWAL AND CANCELLATION OF THE OFFERING WITHOUT NOTICE.

1. SUMMARY OF THE OFFERING

The following summary is qualified in its entirety by the detailed information and financial statements appearing elsewhere in this Memorandum.

The Company

Newcorp, Inc. is a California corporation incorporated in 1991 for the purpose of developing and marketing tele-presence for entertainment, education, and commerce. The company is a development, start-up, or seed-stage company with no operating history or developed product.

The proceeds of this Offering will be used to develop a prototype tele-presence program for entertainment, to determine costs and price of high volume tele-presence presentation, to select a target market for an initial tele-presence theater, and to engage in further capital raising activities as required.

Offices of the Company are located at 8792 Pasodor Ct., San Luis Obispo, CA 93401. The Company telephone number is (805) 562-2990. Inquiries regarding this Offering should be directed to Jake Z. Jones, President.

The Offering

Securities Offered: 100,000 shares of no parcommon stock. The shares will be sold only in four units of 25,000 shares each.

Offering Price: $1.00 per share (1)

Shares outstanding prior to this offering: 300,000

Shares to be outstanding this Offering: 400,000 (2)

(1) As of the date of this Offering the Company was arbitrarily valued by the Board of Directors at $300,000. The amount represents the value of six months of research to determine the state of art of tele-presence, goodwill, initial marketing planning, business plans, copyrighted script material for a prototype show, and the unrealized commercial value of the tele-presence product idea. The

amount also includes $24,000 cash investment and $4,000 of computer equipment invested.

(2) If all 100,000 shares are sold, the Company will have increased its value by $100,000, but the investors in the Offering will have suffered a dilution of 74% of tangible investment since most of the Company assets are not tangible.

Closing

The closing of the Offering ("Closing") is to take place on or before June 30, 1989 or earlier at the discretion of the Board of Directors.

Use of Proceeds

The proceeds of this Offering will be used to develop a prototype tele-presence program for entertainment, to determine costs and price of high-volume tele-presence presentation, to select a target market for an initial tele-presence theater, and to engage in further capital raising activities as required.

Risk Factors

Investment in the shares is speculative and involves a high degree of risk. The risk is created by dependence upon certain key employees, by potential competition by companies much larger than the Company, by the uncertainty of demand for the product, and by potential infringement of the Company's copyrighted materials. Section 4, Risk Factors, discusses the risks in more detail and it should be read carefully by all potential investors before making a decision to invest in the shares.

2. THE COMPANY

Newcorp, Inc. is a California corporation incorporated in 1991 for the purpose of developing and marketing tele-presence for entertainment, education, and commerce. The company is a development, start-up, or seed-stage company with no operating history or developed product.

The proceeds of this Offering will be used to develop a prototype tele-presence program for entertainment, to determine cost and price of high-volume tele-presence presentation, to select a target market for an initial tele-presence theater, and to engage in further capital raising activities as required.

There is one stockholder in the Company, its founder and President, Jake Z. Jones. Jake Jones has served as CEO of Superdisk, Inc. and he has entered into an employment agreement with Newcorp, Inc. with full disclosure of his working arrangement to Superdisk, Inc. and Newcorp, Inc. Jones will spend half his time working for Superdisk and half his time working for Newcorp for the next three years, upon successful funding of this Offering and if the Company honors all the terms of his employment agreement.

Offices of the Company are located at 8792 Pasodor Ct., San Luis Obispo, CA 93401. The Company telephone number is (805) 562-2990. Inquiries regarding this Offering should be directed to Jake Z. Jones, President.

3. FINANCES

The Company has no operating history and the successful sale of the Offering is required to produce initial working capital for the Company, which has minimal tangible assets. The Company has no debt, and it has no established lines of credit or vendor relations. Cash invested in the Company as of the date of this Offering is $24,000 and it has $4,000 of tangible computer equipment. It is highly unlikely that additional stock will have to be sold before the Company reaches breakeven profit, and investors in this Offering will have to make further investment or suffer dilution of ownership.

4. RISK FACTORS

The following risk factors should be carefully considered before purchasing the shares of common stock offered by this Memorandum.

1. *Dependence upon Key Personnel.* The Company is dependent upon key employees. The loss of key employees would have a material, adverse effect upon the Company.

2. *Competition.* The market for visual entertainment contains many successful competitors in movies, television, and video. There are no known competitors producing tele-presence at this time, but there can be no assurance that competition will not develop.

3. *No Assurance of Market for Product.* There can be no assurance that the tele-presence product, if developed successfully, will be able to be sold profitably.

4. *Lack of Protection for Proprietary Rights.* The Company cannot be assured that such copyrights as it may obtain on its programs will not be infringed.

5. *Dependence Upon Subcontractors for Product Display Machines.* The Company does not plan to manufacture tele-presence equipment and it is dependent upon a single Japanese supplier for that display equipment. No contracts have been entered into between the Company and its potential supplier, and no other suppliers are known to exist.

6. *Absence of Prior Public Market.* No public market for the Company's common stock presently exists and no assurance can be given that an active trading market for such a stock will, at any time, develop. As such, an investment in the Company is illiquid and investors may be required to hold their investment indefinitely.

7. *Dividends.* It is not expected that the Company will pay cash dividends in the foreseeable future.

8. *Concentration of Control.* The Company is controlled by Jake Jones and it is likely that he will be able to maintain control of the Company and its Board of Directors for the foreseeable future. Thus, a purchaser of the shares cannot expect to exert any control or influence over the management of the Company.

9. *Dilution.* The investor will incur immediate dilution upon purchasing shares in the Offering. Further sale of stock may be required to fund the Company resulting in further dilution. See Section 5, Dilution.

10. *Arbitrary Offering Price.* The price of the stock of the Company has been arbitrarily established by the Board of Directors and such price may not bear any relationship to the Company's assets or future prospects or any other recognized basis of valuation.

11. *Lack of Financial History.* The Company has had no operations, and, therefore, it has no financial history to report.

12. *Restriction on Resale of Stock.* All of the Company's shares of common stock to be issued hereby will be outstanding and are "restricted securities," as that term is defined in Rule 144 under the Securities Act of 1933, as amended.

5. DILUTION

Net Offering Proceeds	$100,000
Tangible Net Worth Prior to Offering	$ 4,000
Net Worth After Offering	$104,000
Shares Outstanding Prior to Offering	$300,000
Shares Outstanding After Offering	400,000
Net Worth per Share After Offering	$ 0.26
Dilution per Share	$ 0.74

6. USE OF PROCEEDS

The proceeds of this Offering will be used to develop a proto-type tele-presence program for entertainment, to determine costs and price of high-volume tele-presence presentation, to select a target market for an initial tele-presence theater, and to engage in further capital raising activities as required.

7. DIVIDEND POLICY

The dividend policy shall be determined by the Board of Directors of the Company. At the time of this Offering, no plan exists to declare any dividends in the foreseeable future.

8. CAPITALIZATION

Total Tangible Assets	$ 4,000
Non-tangible Assets	$296,000
Total Liabilities	$ 0
Net Worth Prior to Offering	$300,000
Net Worth After Offering	$400,000
Current Shares Outstanding	300,000
Shares Outstanding After Offering	400,000

9. BUSINESS

The business of the Company is to develop profitable commercial applications for the emerging technology of tele-presence. The initial applications for tele-presence will be directed at the entertainment industry. As the Company obtains a surplus of capital above its needs to service the entertainment industry, tele-presence applications in robotic manufacturing and mining will be developed.

The strategic decision to commence operations in the entertainment industry is a function of low investment barrier compared to manufacturing or mining and a function of potentially high rates of capital formation and high liquidity.

The drawback to the entertainment industry is that successful operations will be quickly copied and the strategic advantage of being first will become less with the passage of time. Therefore, as soon as the company expands to its maximum size in the entertainment industry, it expects to commence investment in manufacturing and mining applications for the technology. Tele-presence is particularly well suited to extending operator intelligence into environments not economically accessible to human operators, e.g., undersea and space.

A key strategy of the company is to use existing technology rather than develop the tele-presence technology itself. The Company will produce software, tele-present shows, and do contract remote manipulation for manufacturing and mining, but it will not get involved in research and development of the tele-presence hardware. Such a strategy is designed to keep the company liquid and profitable, but it will always invite competition. The company will strive to do better than the competition by offering better service and by gaining early market share advantage.

10. MARKETING

The Company's tele-presence product will initially sell in the video arcade segment of the entertainment industry. As customers become accustomed to the new video technology, it is possible that the market can widen to compete with movies and video tapes.

The video arcade segment of the market has stabilized at a high level after a period of rapid growth. One of the users of the funds raised in this Offering will be to accurately gauge the size and distribution of the video arcade market. The market is estimated to be in the range of $250 million to $750 million per year.

The chief characteristic of the market is its extremely broad distribution. Since large theaters are not required, video arcades are found in most shopping malls and in many movie theater lobbies. Another central characteristic of the market is the youthful and masculine group that compose a vast majority of its customer base. The video games are very action oriented and interactive. Play time is brief, several minutes, and it sell for twenty five cents to a dollar a play with the vast majority of play at the lower end of the scale.

While the end users of the tele-presence product will be young men, the customers will be proprietors of small video arcades. Research must be done to determine what drives the purchasing decisions of this group of businessmen, but it can be logically assumed that leasing of the equipment and shows will be required to sell to this customer base.

The major application of tele-presence entertainment will be short, highly realistic, action clips. These clips will be about two to three minutes in length on subjects such as cliff climbing, hot air ballooning, fighter jet flight, stunt flying, driver's seat racing at the Indy 500, and drag racing.

The unique edge of tele-presence in this market will be its extremely gratifying visual realism, which will set it apart from even the most realistic interactive games. It is expected that the novelty of the experience will attract viewers who are becoming bored with the repetition of the arcade video games.

The major trend in the industry is toward increasing realism. Tele-presence will set a new, much higher, standard for realism in the video game industry. Because it is not interactive, at least in its introduction, it will complement rather than replace the competition.

The target market for tele-presence will be diversion of dollars spent for video games to short, thrillingly realistic, tele-presence displays. Assuming that the average distribute of video games is twenty per arcade and that the tele-presence display obtains average use, the market potential is 5% of the video arcade market or an estimated at $12.5 million to $37.5 million. Further assuming a three-way split between the leasing company, the arcade owner, and the tele-presence company, the sales goal for the Company is initially $4.15 million to $12.45 million.

The competition are the manufacturers of interactive computer video games. The competition is well financed and well established. The Company intends to complement the product offerings of the competition. It is not expected that the 5% of the market taken by the Company in its plan will cause the competition to enter the tele-presence market, which is quite different technically from their current product line. The impact of the Company on any given competitor is expected to range from less than 1% to 2% of the total market, and no more than 5% of their individual share.

Methods of sales and marketing will be determined by further research funded by the proceeds of this Offering, including test marketing of the prototype system.

11. PROPERTY, EQUIPMENT, AND EMPLOYEES

The company occupies an office in the home of principal founder of the Company. It is expected that successful closing of the seed capital Offering will allow the Company to obtain a small office with attached lab space for development of the prototype. Until the first equipment is available from Japan, the current office space offers the Company a way in which to minimize its overhead while doing marketing and sales research.

The company currently owns a MacIntosh Plus computer with a modem, an Imagewriter II letter-quality printer, and a thirty megabyte CMS external hard disk drive. It also owns software for desk top publishing of advertising materials, spreadsheet software, database software, communications software, graphics software, and word processing software. The Company also owns an IBM Selectric II typewriter and minimal office furniture.

The Company has no full-time employees. It is expected that the President will become the first full-time employees of the Company. A Vice-president of Marketing and Sales will be hired on a consulting basis until the prototype is developed, at which time he will be come a full-time employee.

The Company is located in San Luis Obispo, California. San Luis Obispo is a destination of choice for many professional people and it serves as the home for the California Polytechnic University (Cal Poly). CalPoly is an excellent source of trained technical people from part-time lab assistants to full-time PhD-level scientists and engineers. San Luis Obispo is located midway between Los Angeles and San Francisco, which locates both of those vast markets within an easy three- to four-hour drive.

12. MANAGEMENT

The Management of the Company is to be established. It is expected that some of the investors in the Offering will become members of the Board of Directors and employees of the Company as consultants.

The President of the Company, Jake Z. Jones, has twenty years of experience in forming and managing small businesses.

Mr. Jones has served as President, General Partner, Director, and Chairman of the Board of various corporations (both public and private, for profit and nonprofit public benefit), and partnerships.

This experience includes twelve years as President of Superdisk, Inc., a company that produces several high-technology computer peripherals. Prior to founding Superdisk, Mr. Jones was General Partner of Electro Mag.

Mr. Jones's entire career has been involved with the production and sales of new electronic products.

Mr. Jones is active in the nonprofit Society for Fair Business Practices, where he served as Chairman between 1981 and 1987.

Mr. Jones holds a BSEE from Brigham Young University, 1961. He is listed in *Who's Who in the West.* Mr. Jones is a registered Professional Engineer and a long-standing member of the Society of Professional and Registered Engineers.

13. OTHER TRANSACTIONS

At present, the Company has not entered into any transactions or agreements with other entities. It is expected, however, that the Company will enter agreements with one or more Japanese manufacturers of the tele-presence equipment required for its products.

14. PRINCIPAL STOCKHOLDERS

Name and address of Each Officer and Director

	% Ownership Prior to the Offering	*Shares*
Jake Z. Jones 8792 Pasodor Ct. San Luis Obispo, CA 93401	100.00%	300,000

15. OTHER AGREEMENTS AFFECTING STOCK OWNERSHIP

Presently, there are no other agreements, options, or plans to form other agreements affecting stock ownership.

16. DESCRIPTION OF COMMON STOCK

The currently authorized capital stock of the Company consists of 500,000 shares of Common Stock having no par value. Holders of the shares are entitled to one vote for each share of stock.

The presently issued and outstanding shares of Common Stock of the Company are fully paid and nonassessable. The shares of stock of the Company offered in this Memorandum, upon sale and issuance, as set forth herein, will also be validly issued, fully paid and nonassessable. All shares of Common Stock are entitled to share equally in dividends from sources legally available, if and when declared by the Board of Directors. The Company does not anticipate paying cash dividends in the foreseeable future. The shares of common stock are entitled to share equally in the assets of the Company available for distribution upon liquidation of the Company whether voluntary or involuntary.

Upon completion of this Offering at maximum available for subscription, there will be 400,000 shares of stock outstanding, all of which will be "restricted" securities, as such term is defined under the Securities Act of 1933, as amended.

17. RESTRICTIONS ON TRANSFERABILITY

Each investor will be required to represent and warrant, among other things, that he is acquiring the shares for investment for his own account and will also be required to agree, among other things, not to attempt to assign, sell, or make any disposition of his shares, in whole or in part, unless such shares are the subject of an effective registration statement under the Securities Act of 1933, as amended, and under any applicable state securities laws, or unless the investor has first delivered to the Company a written opinion of counsel, satisfactory to the Company, that the assignment, sale, or other disposition of such shares would neither constitute nor result in any violation of the federal or any state securities laws. A legend to this effect will be placed upon any certificate evidencing shares and will be noted in the Company records.

As indicated above, any shares purchased hereunder will be subject to substantial legal restrictions on their transferability. Possible bases for such transfer in the future are the following:

Resale Under Rule 144

Theoretically, the shares could be sold in limited amounts through unsolicited broker's transactions pursuant to Rule 144 of the SEC after the shares have been beneficially owned by an investor for at least two years, if certain information about the Company is publicly available at the time of resale, and if various other conditions of the Rule are satisfied. In light of the likelihood that no public market for the shares will exist and that information about the Company, as prescribed by Rule 144, will not be publicly available, it is unlikely that the requirements of Rule 144 could be met for resales of the shares. The Company is not under any obligation to, and it does not intend to, make information about the Company, as prescribed by Rule 144, publically available.

Resale by Registration

Shares could be sold at any time, if the Company were to register, or to obtain a registration exemption under Regulation A of the SEC for, the sale by the investor (except that the maximum amount that could be sold under Regulation A during any twelve-month period would be $100,000 for each investor and $300,000 for all investors as a group). The Company is not under any obligation to, and it does not intend to, register the shares.

Resale Under Administrative Doctrines

The shares may be sold if, in the written opinion of counsel satisfactory to the Company, the proposed transaction would be permissible under administrative doctrines of the SEC in effect at the time of the resale and under any applicable securities law of any state. It is not possible to forecast the administrative doctrines that might exist at any future date of a proposed sale of the shares. The Company is not under any obligation to, and does not intend to, assist in compliance with, or make available any exemption from registration under the federal or state securities laws in connection with resales by any investor at any time. The restrictions and methods for reselling the shares are subject to broad discretionary powers of authorities administering the federal and state securities laws, including the powers, among others, to modify and rescind rules and, in the case of state authorities, to withdraw exemptions accorded by state statutes. There are many detailed requirements of such rules and regulations that must be satisfied before such rules and regulations can be used. Each prospective investor, therefore, should consult his own attorney for additional details regarding the applications of these laws with respect to the investor's own circumstances.

18. OFFERING

The Company is offering 100,000 shares of the Company's common stock at a price of $1.00 per share. This offer is intended to be exempt from federal and, where possible, state requirements concerning the registration of securities, in reliance upon an exemption available for nonpublic offerings. Further, it is intended that this offer will satisfy the conditions of Rule 504 of the SEC or Section 4(2) of the Securities Act of 1933, as amended. Therefore, the shares are being offered only to persons whom the officers of the Company have reasonable grounds to believe, and actually believe, prior to making a sale (1) are able to evaluate the merits and risks of an investment in the shares, or (2) are able to bear the economic risks of an investment in the shares, and prior to subscribing to purchase the shares, are represented by a purchaser representative who is capable of evaluating the merits and risks of an investment in the shares. Each prospective investor must execute an Investor

Questionnaire, in the form accompanying this Memorandum, representing to the Company, among other matters, that such investor's annual gross income is at least $50,000 and that he has a net worth of at least $100,000 (exclusive of home, furnishings, and personal automobiles), or no income requirement and a net worth of of at least $200,000 (exclusive of home, furnishings, and personal automobiles), and that the investment will not exceed 10% of the purchaser's net worth.

Each prospective investor will also be required to execute a Subscription Agreement, in the form accompanying this Memorandum or as otherwise approved by the Company. Prior to acceptance by the Company of any Subscription Agreement, each prospective investor must (1) if required by the Company, appoint, acknowledge in writing, and consult with a qualified offeree representative; (2) give such assurances as the Company may require with respect to his ability to bear the economic risks of investment in the shares; (3) satisfy any qualifications under the California Corporations Code or any other applicable state securities law; (4) acknowledge receipt and review of this Memorandum and other such information as the Company may furnish; and (5) sign a written agreement, contained in the Subscription Agreement, that any shares acquired pursuant to this Offering shall not be sold without registration thereof under the Securities Act of 1933, as amended, any successor law, and state securities laws or an exemption therefrom. See Section 17, Restrictions on Transferability.

The full purchase price is payable upon execution by a prospective investor of his Subscription Agreement. A Subscription Agreement, when executed by the prospective investor and submitted to the Company, constitutes a firm offer to purchase the shares specified and is irrevocable. All funds paid for shares under Subscription Agreements accepted by the Company will immediately become the property of and be useable by the Company. The Company has the unconditional right to reject any Subscription or to close the Offering. This Offering will terminate upon the earlier of (1) the acceptance of subscription for 100,000 shares or (2) June 30, 1991. There will be no commissions paid by the Company in connection with this Offering.

A prospective investor who desires to subscribe for shares would complete and execute the Investor Questionnaire and the Subscription Agreement that accompany this Memorandum and deliver them to the Company, together with his payment for the shares. Within thirty days after receipt of the Subscription, the Company will notify each prospective investor as to whether his Subscription Agreement has been accepted or rejected or whether additional information is required from such prospective investor. If the Company rejects a prospective investor's Subscription Agreement, all funds received from such investor will be promptly returned to him, without interest and without deduction for expenses.

The Company is unaware of any person, including any affiliate, who intends to finance any portion of the purchase price of shares to be acquired in the Offering. The proceeds from this Offering will not be used, directly or indirectly, to enable anyone to purchase shares.

19. LEGAL PROCEEDINGS

There is no litigation that is currently pending against the Company or to which the Company is a party.

20. ADDITIONAL INFORMATION

Any further information that may be needed by prospective investors to verify the information contained in this Memorandum or to aid in understanding the Company and this Offering will be provided by the Company upon written request by a prospective investor, or his Offeree Representative, if any, provided that (i) the Company possesses such information, (ii) that such information is not of such a confidential nature that it may damage the interests of the Company (in which case a prospective investor may be required to sign an agreement of confidentiality), or the Company can acquire such information without unreasonable effort or expense. Request for such information should be directed to Jake Z. Jones, President, 8792 Pasodor Ct., San Luis Obispo, CA 93401, telephone: (805) 562-2990.

THIS CONSTITUTES THE FULL AND COMPLETE OFFERING. FOLLOWING ARE:

Exhibit A - Subscription Agreement
Exhibit B - Purchaser Representative Questionnaire
Exhibit C - Investor Questionnaire

EXHIBIT A

NEWCORP, INC.
SUBSCRIPTION AGREEMENT

I hereby acknowledge receipt of a copy of the Private Placement Memorandum dated April 1, 1991 (the "Memorandum"), for Newcorp, Inc., a corporation organized under the laws of the State of California (the "Company"), and relating to the offering of 100,000 shares of common stock in the Company (the "Shares"), at a price of $1.00 per share, with four units of 25,000 shares each at $25,000 per unit.

I hereby subscribe for:

_____ units of $25,000 of 25,000 shares each.

The total purchase price for the units subscribed is _____ . Attached hereto are my (1) check payable to Newcorp, Inc. in an amount equal to the total purchase price for the units listed above, and (2) my completed and signed Investor Questionnaire.

In conenction with this subscription, I hereby make the following acknowledgments and representations:

1. I understand the Offering is being made pursuant to the exemption from registration with the Securities and Exchange Commission (the "SEC") afforded by Section 4(2) of the Securities Act of 1933, as amended, and Rule 504 adopted thereunder by the SEC relating to transactions by an issuer not involving any public offering. Consequently, the materials submitted have not been subject to review and comment by the staff of the SEC.

2. I have, and my purchaser representative (if any) has, carefully read the memorandum and fully understood all matters set forth therein and in this Subscription Agreement.

3. I have, and my purchaser representative (if any) has, had an opportunity to question, and to receive answers from, the Officers of the Company and to obtain any additional information necessary to verify the accuracy of the information contained in this memorandum (and any amendments, supplements, or exhibits hereto), or any other supplemental information which I or my purchaser representative (if any) deem relevant to make an informed investment decision as to participation in the Offering.

4. I have, or my purchaser representative (if any) has, sufficient knowledge and experience in business and financial matters in general, and I am, together with my purchaser representative (if any), capable of utilizing the information regarding purchase of shares in the Company; and I am capable of bearing all the economic risks involved in this investment with full knowledge that this investment could result in a total loss to me.

5. The Shares are being acquired by the undersigned solely for his own account, for investment purposes only, and are not being purchased with a view to, or in connection with, any resale, distribution, subdivision, or fractionalization of the Shares; the undersigned has no agreement or other arrangement with any person to sell, transfer, or pledge any of the Shares; and the undersigned has no plans to enter into any such agreement or arrangement.

6. I have either (1) a present net worth of at least $200,000 or more (excluding home, furnishings, and automobiles) or (2) will have during my current tax year gross income of at least $50,000 and a present net worth of at least $100,000 (excluding home, furnishings, and automobiles), and that this investment does not exceed 10% of my net worth.

7. I understand that the offering of the Shares has not been registered under the Securities Act of 1933, as amended (the "Act"), and that you are selling the Shares to me in reliance upon an exemption from the registration requirements of the Act pursuant

to Section 4(2) of the Act and Regulation D adopted under the Act and exemptions from registration under certain state securities laws.

8. I agree that I will not transfer the Shares in the absence of an effective registration statement relating thereto under the Act and under any applicable state securities law; and I further agree that the certificate which will be issued representing the Shares may be endorsed with the following legend:

"This certificate and the interests represented hereby have not been registered under the Securities Act of 1933, as amended, or under any applicable state securities law, and may not be transferred in the absence of an effective registration statement relating thereto under the Securities Act of 1933, as amended, or any successor law, and under any applicable state securities law, or in opinion of counsel satisfactory to Newcorp, Inc. to the effect that such registration is not required under such Act, as amended, or any applicable state law."

9. I understand that in addition to the restrictions on transfer contained in the legend to be placed upon the certificate representing the Shares, I must bear the economic risk of the investment for an indefinite period because the Shares have not been registered under the Act or under any applicable state securities law and; no federal or state agency has passed on or made any recommendation or endorsement with respect to the Shares; and, therefore, the Shares are subject to restrictions on transfer such that they may not be sold or otherwise transferred unless they are registered under the Act, or any successor law, and any applicable state securities law or any exemption from such registration is available. I understand the Company is not under any obligation, and does not have any present intention, to file a registration statement under such Act, or successor law or to comply with Regulation A or any other exemption under such Act, or any successor law, or under any applicable state securities law for such purposes.

10. (a)   I have _____ /have not _____ (place check after the applicable statement) employed a purchaser representative to assist or advise me in connection with evaluating the risks of the prospective investment.

(b)   If a purchaser representative has been employed, following is his or her name, address and occupation:

_____   _____

Name

                                   _____

_____

Occupation   _____

                                   Address

11. I understand the Company shall have the right to accept or reject this Subscription Agreement in whole or in part in its sole and absolute discretion.

12. This Subscription Agreement shall be governed by the laws of the State of California.

13. The representations, warranties, and agreements herein contained are made and given to induce you to sell and issue the Shares to me, and each constitutes a material portion of the consideration therefore.

14. This subscription is form and irrevocable.

The undersigned hereby direct the Shares be held as follows:

_____ Individual Ownership

_____ Joint Tenants—State Names: _____

_____

_____ Tenant in Common—State Names: _____

_____

(If two or more persons are purchasing Shares, each should sign below.)

IN WITNESS WHEREOF, the undersigned has executed this Subscription Agreement this _____ day of _____ , 1991.

_____	_____
Signature	Signature
_____	_____
Name	Name
_____	_____
Social Security Number	Social Security Number
_____	_____
Residence	Residence
_____	_____
City	City
_____	_____
State and Zip Code	State and Zip Code
_____	_____
Area Code and Telephone Number	Area Code and Telephone Number

ACCEPTED:
Newcorp, Inc.

By: _____

Title: _____

Date: _____

EXHIBIT B

PURCHASER REPRESENTATIVE QUESTIONNAIRE

Name of Purchaser: _____

Proposed Investment: Purchase of Stock issued by Newcorp, Inc. (the "Company") pursuant to the Private Placement Memorandum dated April 1, 1991.

Please complete the following questionnaire fully, attaching additional sheets if necessary.

1. Name: _____

   Age: _____

   Business Address: _____

2. Present occupation or position, indicating period of such practice or employment and field of professional specialization if any:

   _____

3. List any business or professional education, including degrees received, if any: _____

   _____

4.   Have you had prior experience in advising clients with respect to investments of this type: _____ Yes _____ No

5.   List any professional license or registrations, including bar admissions, accounting certifications, real estate brokerage licenses, and SEC or state broker-dealer registrations, held by you:

    _____

    _____

6.   Describe generally any business, financial or investment experience that would help you evaluate the merits and risks of this investment: _____

    _____

7.   Please state how long you have known the Purchaser and in what capacity: _____

    _____

8.   Neither I nor any of my affiliates presently have any material relationship with the Company or any of its affiliates, no such material relationship has existed at any time during the previous two years, and no such material relationship is mutually understood to be contemplated with the Company, except:

(a) _____

(b) If a material relationship is disclosed in subparagraph (a) above, indicate the amount of compensation received or to be received as the result of such a relationship:

_____

9. In advising the Purchaser in connection with the prospective investment referenced above, I will be relying in part on the Purchaser's own expertise in certain areas: _____ Yes _____ No

10. In advising the Purchaser in connection with the prospective investment referenced above, I will be relying in part on the expertise of an additional offeree representative or representatives.

_____ Yes _____ No

If "Yes" please give the name and addresses of such additional representative or representatives:

_____

11. I understand that the Company will be relying on the accuracy and completeness of my responses to the following questions, and I represent and warrant to the Company as follows:

(i) I am acting as Purchaser Representative for the above named Purchaser in connection with the Purchaser's prospective investment referenced above;

(ii) The answers to the above questions are complete and correct and may be relied upon by the Company in determining whether the offering with respect to which I have executed this questionnaire is exempt from registration under the Securities Act of 1933, pursuant to Regulation D or otherwise;

(iii) I will notify the Company immediately of any material change in any statement made here in occurring prior to the closing of any purchase by the Purchaser of any interest in the proposed investment;

(iv) I am not an affiliate, director, officer, or other employee of the Company or any subsidiaries or affiliates, or a beneficial owner of 10% or more of any class of the equity securities of the Company or any of its subsidiaries, nor will I have any similar interest in the Company;

(v) I have disclosed to the Purchaser in writing prior to the Purchaser's acknowledgment of me as his Purchaser Representative, any material relationship with the Company or any of its affiliates disclosed in response to question 8 above; and

(vi) I personally (or, if I have checked "yes" in question 9 or 10 above, together with the Purchaser or the additional Purchaser Representative or Representatives indicated above) have such knowledge or experience in financial and business matters that I am capable of evaluating the merits and risks of the Purchaser's prospective investment in the Company.

(vii) I further acknowledge that I have received a copy of the Memorandum setting forth information relating to the Company and terms and conditions of an investment therein, as well as any other information I deem necessary or appropriate to evaluate the merits and risks of investment in the Company. I acknowledge that the Company has made available to me the opportunity to obtain additional information to verify the accuracy of the information contained in the Memorandum and to evaluate the merits and risks of an investment in the Company. I further acknowledge that I had the opportunity to ask questions of and receive answers from the Company concerning the terms and conditions of the Offering and the information contained in the Memorandum.

IN WITNESS whereof, I have executed this Questionnaire this _____ day of _____ , 1991.

_____

Signature of Purchaser
Representative

EXHIBIT C

INVESTOR QUESTIONNAIRE

Newcorp, Inc.
8792 Pasodor Court
San Luis Obispo, CA 93401

Attention: Mr. Jake Z. Jones, President

The information contained herein is being furnished to you in order to assure you that the undersigned meets the standards for investors under Regulation D promulgated under the Securities Act of 1933 (the "Act"). The undersigned understands that (1) you will rely upon the information contained herein for purposes of such determination, (2) the securities will not be registered under the Act in reliance upon the exemption from registration provided by Section 4(2) of the Act and Regulation D, and (3) this questionnaire is not an offer to sell securities to the undersigned.

The undersigned further represents to you that (1) the information contained herein is complete and accurate and may be relied upon by you, and (2) the undersigned will notify you immediately of any material change in any of such information occurring prior to the purchase of such securities, if any purchase is made, by the undersigned.

THE UNDERSIGNED UNDERSTANDS AND AGREES THAT, ALTHOUGH THIS QUESTIONNAIRE WILL BE KEPT STRICTLY CONFIDENTIAL, THE ISSUER OF ANY SECURITIES PURCHASED BY THE UNDERSIGNED MAY PRESENT THIS QUESTIONNAIRE TO SUCH PARTIES AS

IT DEEMS ADVISABLE IF CALLED UPON TO ESTABLISH THE AVAILABILITY UNDER ANY FEDERAL OR STATE SECURITIES LAWS OF ANY EXEMPTION FROM REGIS- TRATION OF THE PRIVATE PLACEMENT.

THIS LETTER IS NOT AN OFFER TO SELL SECURI- TIES BUT MERELY A REQUEST FOR INFORMATION PURSUANT TO REGULATION D OF THE SECURITIES AND EXCHANGE COMMISSION.

The undersigned will, upon request, furnish such additional statements or information concerning his financial position and business experience as may be required to qualify him as an "Of- feree."

Please complete, sign, date, and return one copy of this ques- tionnaire to: Mr. Jake Z. Jones, President, Newcorp, Inc., 8792 Pasodor Court, San Luis Obispo, CA 93401. All questions should be answered with respect to you personally, disregarding any sepa- rate experience, assets, or liabilities of your spouse or other family members.

PLEASE PRINT OR TYPE

1. Name: _____

   Birth Date: _____ Social Security Number: _____

   Marital Status: _____ Citizenship: _____

2. Home Address: _____

    _____

    Home Phone: (___) – ___   Other Phone: (___) – ___

3. Are you acting for your own account? _____ Yes _____ No

4. Your positions or occupations during the past 5 years (and the inclusive dates of each) are as follows:
    (Note: What is sought is a sufficient description to enable the Issuer to determine the extent of vocationally related experience in financial and business matters.)

Position or Occupation	Firm Name	Period
_____	_____	_____
_____	_____	_____
_____	_____	_____
_____	_____	_____

5. Degrees and year degrees were received are as follows:

_____

_____

6. My income from all sources for the latest calendar year was more than:

_____ $30,000   _____ $40,000   _____ $50,000

_____ $75,000   _____ $100,000   _____ $250,000

  (a) What percentage of your income as shown above was derived from sources other than salary? _____

  (b) Approximately what percentage of your income as shown above remained after the payment of all federal, state, and local taxes, and after payment of all ordinary and necessary living expenses? _____

7. What was your tax bracket for the latest complete calendar year (i.e., the taxable rate imposed upon the last dollar of taxable income reported in your federal tax return?).

_____

8. Is your average yearly income (from all sources anticipated for the 3-year period ending with the current calendar year) in excess of:

_____ $30,000   _____ $40,000   _____ $50,000

_____ $75,000   _____ $100,000   _____ $1,000,000

(a) My net worth is _____ .

(b) What percentage of your net worth as shown is comprised of personal residence, furnishings and automobiles?

_____

(c) What percentage of your net worth as shown is comprised of of cash, fungible securities, or assets readily convertible to cash?

_____

9. Do you have any other investments or contingent liabilities which you reasonably anticipate could cause you to require cash equal to or in excess of your liquid assets?

_____ Yes _____ No

10. Investment experience:

(a) Please indicate the frequency of your investment in marketable securities:

_____ often   _____ occasionally   _____ seldom   _____ never

(b) Please indicate if you have ever invested in:

____ options ____ commodities futures ____ securities on margin

(c) Please indicate the frequency of your investment in un-marketable securities:

____ often ____ occasionally ____ seldom ____ never

Year	Type of Securities	Issuer	Business of Issuer	Amount Invested

11. Please indicate in the space provided below any additional information that you think might be helpful in enabling the Issuer to determine that your knowledge or experience in fi-

nancial and business matters is sufficient to enable you to evaluate the merits and risks of this investment:

_____

_____

_____

To the best of my information and belief, the above supplied by the undersigned is true and correct in all respects.

IN WITNESS WHEREOF, I have executed this questionnaire

this _____ day of, _____ , 1989.

_____
Signature of Investor

Index